Shipping I ~

MA (Oxford) Ll   ᶜCIArb

Asso   .ycssor of the Common Law

University of Exeter Law School

2nd edition.

I have sought to state the law as of 1 June 2021.

Lizzie R Wilce, one of several ships whose master was part of the author's extended family. With thanks to Peter Tamblyn.

Outline Contents

Detailed Contents

Chapter 1 – A Very Brief History

Introducing the Admiralty Court and its law

Origins of the High Court

Communities usually found a way of resolving their disputes, and their practices often firmed into local custom. This was true across England until it was decided that all communities should be regulated by the same law, common to them all, with beginnings in the 12th century. The king toured the country, resolving disputes in what came to be the King's Bench. It was more convenient for the king's treasure and revenue service to remain in one place, so the Exchequer came to be located in Westminster. (The Exchequer was named after the chequered table used to reckon accounts.) It was not always practical for litigants to follow the king around the country, and so the Magna Carta required another fixed court for ordinary business not involving the king, and this gave rise to the Common Bench or Court of Common Pleas, also in Westminster. In time, the King's Bench stopped touring and resided there also. Meanwhile, it was possible to petition the king, asking him to deliver justice by making good any defects in the law. This came to be administered by the Chancery, originally the king's secretariat, which developed a set of rules known as equity.

So it was that the one room of Westminster Hall came to contain the King's Bench, the Court of Common Pleas, and the Chancery, divided by wooden bars at which stood the pleaders. (The Exchequer was off in a side room.) These courts developed their procedures and laws, sometimes in cooperation, often in competition as they vied for business and influence. Eventually in 1875 they were consolidated into a single court system, although some of the older names (like King's Bench and Chancery) were retained for the divisions of the High Court, to mark different areas of specialism. Although England and Wales now knows only one law, centuries of opposition still show in some of the tensions or inconsistencies, for example between approaches in common law and equity.

Origins of admiralty law

There were originally three English fleets: North, South, and West. The Admiral of each fleet decided matters of discipline, and given their positions of power and authority it was natural that they came to be concerned with local maritime disputes, often appointing deputies to act as judges. This coalesced into an Admiralty Court, with origins in the 13th century. It applied customary maritime law and Civil Law (unusual aspects of modern admiralty law still reveal this heritage). No doubt this recourse to international sources of law reflected the international nature of shipping business and its international participants in litigation.

As for customary maritime law, early regard was given to the Rolls of Oleron, perhaps written in the 12th century. (These were cited in a Bristol court case in the 14th century, and were included in the Black Book of the Admiralty, an early compendium for practice in the Admiralty Court.) These were framed as a

14

set of judgments delivered by the court in Oleron, an island in the Bay of Biscay off the French Atlantic coast. It sat on an important trade route, and evidently had a strong reputation for maritime dispute resolution. It was part of the Duchy of Aquitaine which from the 12th century for about 200 years fell under English sovereignty.

As for Civil Law, its maritime origins can be traced back through the Rhodian sea law. This was perhaps written around the 9th century as part of the codification in the Greek language of Byzantine law, itself adapted from Code of Justinian (written in Latin). The latter was an authoritative restatement of Roman law in the mid-6th century, which itself makes reference to the maritime law of the Rhodians. (It is not surprising that the Mediterranean should have seen an early development of local custom for resolving maritime disputes, given centuries of shipping trade by the ancient Egyptians and then the Phoenicians.) Justinian's laws generally were revived in the Middle Ages to become the foundation of Civil Law.

In the Admiralty Court, the attorneys were called proctors, and tended to serve an apprenticeship at the court, while the advocates were Doctors of Civil Law from Oxford or Cambridge. Together they formed the Doctors' Commons, which purchased property in London (their own version of an Inn of Court) where they did business and kept a library.

The jurisdiction and fortunes of the Admiralty Court ebbed and flowed over the centuries, in competition with the other courts. In the mid-19th century (common law) barristers and solicitors were allowed to practice in the court, leading to the demise of the Doctors' Commons, and in 1875 the Admiralty Court was subsumed as a specialist court in the King's (currently Queen's) Bench Division. It is now also part of the Business and Property Courts of the High Court of Justice.

The Admiralty Court is presided over by the Admiralty Judge.[1] There is also the Admiralty Registrar, who has the powers of the Admiralty Judge,[2] and who considers whether claims issued in the Admiralty Court should remain there, and if so whether they should be heard by the Registrar or by the Judge (depending on the complexity of the issues and the value of the claim).[3] The Admiralty Judge can refer issues back to the Registrar for determination (for example, the assessment of damages following a trial on liability).[4] The Registrar also liaises with the Admiralty Marshal in respect of the arrest of ships.

Modern admiralty practice

Around 480 million tonnes of cargo passes through British ports every year. Britain imports around 50% of its food, and most of that arrives by ship. Dover is one of the world's busiest passenger ports. The English Channel is the world's busiest shipping lane. Internationally, around 80% of global trade is transported by ship, with English law and London arbitration being the world's top choice for

---

[1] Other judges in the Queen's Bench Division will also hear cases in the Commercial Court and Admiralty Court.

[2] CPR r 61.1(4).

[3] CPR PD 61.2.

[4] CPR PD 61.13.

maritime dispute resolution. English maritime law continues to be of national and international importance.

This book seeks to introduce the main features of English maritime law. It discusses those topics which arise most frequently in practice, exploring key principles along with illustrative detail drawn from the case law. It seeks to reveal the overall shape of English maritime law, making the subject accessible and navigable.

Chapter 2 – Jurisdiction of the Admiralty Court

Which disputes the Admiralty Court can hear

Section 20(2) of the Senior Courts Act 1981 prescribes the list of questions and claims which the Admiralty Court has jurisdiction to hear and determine. In large part this maps onto the scope of the Arrest Convention 1952 (which in turn was modelled on an earlier English statute).[5]

Most of those questions and claims listed in s 20(2) of the Senior Courts Act 1981 refer to ships. So we start with the preliminary question, what is a ship?

What is a ship?

In the case law, a ship has been described as a sea-going vessel, not 'a little boat going out a mile or two' or a rowing boat, but a vessel whose business is 'really and substantially' to go to sea.[6] By statute, a ship is defined as including any description of vessel used in navigation.[7] In turn, a vessel has been described in the case law as every description of watercraft larger than a rowing boat used or capable of being used as a means of transportation on water.[8]

---

[5] *The Eschersheim* [1976] 1 WLR 430 (HL), 436; *The River Rima* [1988] 2 Lloyd's Rep 193 (HL), 196-197.

[6] *Ex p Ferguson* (1871) LR 6 QB 280 (QBD), 291.

[7] Senior Courts Act 1981, s 24(1); CPR r 61.1(2)(k).

[8] *Steedman v Scofield* [1992] 2 Lloyd's Rep 163 (Adm).

As for navigation, this connotes the idea of planned or ordered movement from one place to another. It is not simply 'messing about in boats', as with the directionally disordered play of a jet ski,[9] or hobby sailing in a dinghy on a reservoir.[10] Similarly, it might be too much to describe as 'navigation' a round trip pleasure cruise on a small artificial lake.[11] But it does extend to short pleasure trips up the Exeter canal because this canal does connect with tidal waters and was navigated from the sea to the quay by other ships.[12]

A floating gas beacon is not a ship,[13] nor is a floating crane pontoon.[14] A remotely operated underwater vehicle, carried on a ship and then deployed, is not itself a ship.[15] But a barge can be a ship even though it has no means of its own propulsion.[16]

So in broad terms, the jurisdiction of the Admiralty Court covers sea-going ships navigated in a planned or ordered manner as a means of transportation on water.

---

[9] *R v Goodwin* [2005] EWCA Crim 3184, [2006] 1 WLR 546. Although a jet ski is used on the sea, it is not properly described as sea-going.

[10] *Curtis v Wild* [1991] 4 All ER 172 (QBD).

[11] *Southport Corp v Morriss* [1893] 1 QB 359 (DC).

[12] *Weeks v Ross* [1913] 2 KB 229 (DC).

[13] *The Gas Float Whitton No 2* [1897] AC 337 (HL).

[14] *Merchants' Marine Insurance Co Ltd v North of England P&I Association* (1926) 26 Ll L Rep 201 (CA).

[15] *The Offshore Guardian* [2020] FCA 273 (Australia).

[16] *The Mac* (1882) 7 PD 126 (CA).

Heads of subject-matter jurisdiction under s 20(2)

We can now consider the detailed list of questions and claims about ships which are listed in s 20(2) of the Senior Courts Act 1981. These comprise the jurisdiction of the Admiralty Court.

This list sets out the types of facts which the Admiralty Court can hear argument about. Of course, those facts still need to reveal a cause of action if a claimant is to be successful. That cause of action can come from admiralty law (like salvage), or it can come from the general law, like contract (for example, breach of charter party) or tort (for example, negligent personal injury).

The questions and claims in the list overlap, and risk resembling a random shopping list. This is because of the history of the Admiralty Court over a thousand years, its rivalry with other courts, its influences from continental law, its merging with common law, and the negotiation of international conventions. Nevertheless, it matters which type of case a claimant has, because different heads of jurisdiction have different procedures and remedies.

Here are the heads of jurisdiction:

Any claim to the possession or ownership of a ship or to the ownership of any share in a ship (s 20(2)(a)). For example, a ship owner might have exercised a right of withdrawal under a demise charter party and now seeks to regain possession of the ship from the demise charterer.

Any question arising between the co-owners of a ship as to possession, employment or earnings of that ship (s 20(2)(b)). For example, some co-owners

21

may want to send the ship on a particular voyage which other co-owners do not agree with. One solution might be to give the reluctant co-owners security to the full value of their interest for the safe return of the ship from the proposed voyage.

Any claim in respect of a mortgage of or charge on a ship or any share in the ship (s 20(2)(c)).

Any claim for damage received by a ship (s 20(2)(d)). For example, the damage might have been caused by another ship, or a pier or buoy. More generally, accidents involving ships are investigated by the Marine Accident Investigation Branch.[17] There is also provision for a formal investigation conducted by a wreck commissioner.[18]

Any claim for damage done by a ship (s 20(2)(e)). The damage must be caused by something done by those engaged in the navigation or management of the ship (for example, like a wrongful manoeuvre); the ship must be the instrument by which the damage is done; and the damage must be suffered by a person or property external to the ship (and not suffered by the ship's owners, for example).[19] The commonest example is perhaps collision, but physical contact by the ship is not necessary. For example, damage might be caused by the ship's wash,[20] or it might possibly extend to the financial loss caused by one ship's dangerous

---

[17] Merchant Shipping Act 1995, s 267; Merchant Shipping (Accident Reporting and Investigation) Regulations 2012 (2012/1734).

[18] Merchant Shipping Act 1995, s 268. A wreck commissioner is usually a High Court Judge who presides over a public inquiry. The modern tendency is for accidents to be investigated instead by the Marine Accident Investigation Branch.

[19] *The Rama* [1996] 2 Lloyd's Rep 281 (Adm).

[20] *The Eschersheim* [1976] 1 WLR 430 (HL), 438.

navigation preventing another from fishing.[21] Because the damage must be suffered by a person or property external to the ship, this section does not include personal injury where, for example, a person fell through tarpaulin into the hold of a ship,[22] nor does it include a claim against a ship for damage to cargo carried on that ship.[23] But it does include[24] oil pollution claims against ships,[25] or against the International Oil Pollution Compensation Fund.[26]

Any claim for loss of life or personal injury... (s 20(2)(f)). This must be sustained in consequence of any defect in a ship or its equipment. Or it must be sustained in consequence of the wrongful act, neglect or default of the owners, charterers or persons in possession or control of the ship, or the master or crew or any other person for whose wrongful act the owners, charterers or persons in possession or control are responsible. The wrongful act must be in the navigation or management of the ship, or in loading, carriage or discharge of goods, or the embarkation, carriage or disembarkation of persons. This section can apply, not just to injury suffered on the negligent ship, but also to injury caused by a negligent ship to those on another ship or ashore.

Any claim for loss of or damage to goods carried in a ship (s 20(2)(g)).

---

[21] *The Dagmara and Ama Antxine* [1988] 1 Lloyd's Rep 431 (Adm).

[22] *The Theta* [1894] P 280.

[23] *The Victoria* (1887) 12 PD 105. In that case, ship A, carrying cargo, collided with ship B. The cargo was damaged. Ship A was found solely to blame. This did not amount to damage done by ship A.

[24] Senior Courts Act 1981, s 20(5).

[25] Merchant Shipping Act 1995, s 153.

[26] Merchant Shipping Act 1995, s 175.

Any claim arising out of any agreement relating to the carriage of goods in a ship or to the use or hire of a ship (s 20(2)(h)). This includes damages for breach of charter party or for breach of a bill of lading contract. It cannot relate to carriage in an unidentified ship.[27] And although 'relating to' is a broad term, still, the agreement must be sufficiently connected to (not too remote from) carriage of goods to fall within this section; not so a claim for non-payment of insurance premiums on a cargo carried on a ship.[28]

Any claim in the nature of salvage (s 20(2)(j)). This includes claims under the Salvage Convention 1989, and under any contract for or in relation to salvage services. It also includes services rendered in saving life from a ship.[29] In broad terms, salvage involves a service voluntarily rendered which successfully assists property in danger. We discuss salvage more fully in a later chapter.

Any claim in the nature of towage in respect of a ship or water-borne[30] aircraft (s 20(2)(k)). This includes escort services even where the escort does not make fast to the accompanied ship.[31]

Any claim in the nature of pilotage in respect of a ship or water-borne[32] aircraft (s 20(2)(l)). Pilots are usually seafarers with detailed knowledge of a local

---

[27] *The Lloyd Pacifico* [1995] 1 Lloyd's Rep 54 (Adm).

[28] *The Sandrina* [1985] 1 Lloyd's Rep 181 (HL).

[29] Senior Courts Act 1981, s 20(6).

[30] Senior Courts Act 1981, s 24(1).

[31] *The Leoborg* [1962] 2 Lloyd's Rep 146 (Adm).

[32] Senior Courts Act 1981, s 24(1).

port, employed by the port to board ships and provide a passage plan to bring them safely into the port.

Any claim in respect of goods or materials supplied to a ship for its operation or maintenance (s 20(2)(m)). This extends beyond goods and materials to all 'necessaries', that is, whatever is fit and proper for the service on which the ship is engaged, including the provision of crew.[33] But the goods must be supplied to a particular ship; not so where a contract to supply containers, to carry goods by ship, was made with ship owners, who might use any ship, rather than the contract specifying that the containers were to be used on a particular identified ship.[34]

Any claim in respect of the construction, repair or equipment of a ship, or in respect of dock charges or dues (s 20(2)(n)). There is a difference between equipment, which suggests something more permanent (like anchors and ropes), and supplies which are merely consumables (like fuel oil); supplies are not covered under this section.[35] A repairer may have a possessory lien at common law until they are paid.

Any claim by a master or member of the crew of a ship for wages (s 20(2)(o)). A master includes every person except a pilot having command or charge of a ship.[36] With wage claims against foreign ships, notification might need to be given first to the relevant consul.[37] Defences to wage claims include

---

[33] *The Nore Challenger and Nore Commander* [2001] 2 Lloyd's Rep 103 (Adm).

[34] *The River Rima* [1988] 2 Lloyd's Rep 193 (HL).

[35] *The D'Vora* [1953] 1 WLR 34.

[36] Senior Courts Act 1981, s 24(1).

[37] Consular Relations Act 1968, s 4.

desertion (quitting the ship without intention to return), absence without leave, and gross misconduct or incompetence (such as habitual drunkenness).

Any claim by a master, shipper, charterer or agent in respect of disbursements made on account of a ship (s 20(2)(p)). Such disbursements must relate to the operational aspects of a ship, that is, what is needed to 'keep the ship going', like bunkers. In contrast, a ship can sail without insurance, whose purpose is only to protect the financial interests of the owner. Thus an insurance premium is not a disbursement.[38] The disbursements must be made on account of the ship itself; not so, for example, when money was advanced to buy bunkers which under the charter party were to be paid for by the charterers (not the ship owners).[39]

Any claim arising out of an act which is or is claimed to be a general average act (s 20(2)(q)). A general average act is where an extraordinary sacrifice or expenditure is reasonably incurred for the purpose of preserving property imperilled in the common adventure. The ship owner will have a possessory lien over cargo for its share of the contribution towards general average.[40] We discuss general average more fully in a later chapter.

Any claim arising out of bottomry (s 20(2)(r)). This section is now redundant. Historically, bottomry bonds were used when a ship owner borrowed money which was necessary to fund the voyage, and the bottom of the ship was pledged as security. They were only valid if there was no other way of obtaining finance. Bottomry bonds are no longer used.

---

[38] *The Sea Friends* [1991] 2 Lloyd's Rep 322 (CA).

[39] *The Castlegate* [1893] AC 38 (HL).

[40] *Castle Insurance v Hong Kong Shipping* [1984] AC 226 (PC).

Any claim for the forfeiture or condemnation of a ship or goods... or for the restoration of a ship or goods after seizure, or for droits in Admiralty (s 20(2)(s)). This section applies to goods which are being or have been carried, or have been attempted to be carried in a ship. Forfeiture might apply, for example, when a ship falsely flies a British flag,[41] or for customs and excises offences, such as a ship being adapted for concealing goods.[42] As for droits of Admiralty, these are historical entitlements now vested in the Crown with proceeds being paid into the public purse. They cover such property as wrecks,[43] flotsam (goods lost overboard which float on the sea) and jetsam (when goods are cast into the sea to lighten a ship in danger of sinking).

Additional topics of jurisdiction

The Admiralty Court has further jurisdiction in addition to the list of claims and questions in s 20(2) of the Senior Courts Act 1981, in the following two instances:

By s 20(3) of the Senior Courts Act 1981, its jurisdiction extends to: applications under the Merchant Shipping Acts 1894 to 1979 (for example, concerning ship registration); any action to enforce a claim for damage, loss of life or personal injury arising out of collision, manoeuvres or non-compliance with the

---

[41] Merchant Shipping Act 1894, s 69(1).

[42] Customs and Excise Management Act 1979, s 88.

[43] Finders of wreck must report their finding to the receiver of wreck, or risk criminal conviction: Merchant Shipping Act 1995, s 236. (The receiver is usually an officer of customs and excise, or the coastguard.)

collision regulations; and any action for the limitation of liability. (Limitation of liability is also discussed in a later chapter.)

By s 20(1)(c) of the Senior Courts Act 1981, the Court has any other admiralty jurisdiction which it had immediately before the commencement of the 1981 Act. This might include the power to grant an injunction to prohibit injurious acts taking place on the high seas, for example interfering with another's salvage operations.[44] It might also include 'necessaries', to the extent that these are not otherwise covered by s 20(2). Necessaries need not be absolutely necessary, but are whatever is fit and proper for the service on which the vessel is engaged, whatever the prudent owner would have ordered had they been present at the time.[45] They can be supplied to any ship elsewhere than at the port to which it belongs, unless its owner is domiciled in England.[46]

---

[44] *The Tubantia* [1924] P 78 (Adm).

[45] *Webster v Seekamp* (1821) 4 B & Ald 352; 106 ER 966. In that case, a ship bound for the Mediterranean was coppered. This was not absolutely necessary, but was useful and prudent, and so constituted 'necessaries'.

[46] s 20(1)(c) of the Senior Courts Act 1981 takes us back to the Administration of Justice Act 1956, s 1, which has a similar saving provision, which takes us back again to the Supreme Court of Judicature (Consolidation) Act 1925, s 22(1)(a)(vii), which recites the following jurisdiction. 'Any claim for necessaries supplied to a foreign ship, whether within the body of a county or on the high seas, and, unless it is shown to the court that at the time of the institution of proceedings any owner or part owner of the ship was domiciled in England, any claim for any necessaries supplied to a ship elsewhere than in the port to which the ship belongs.' This in turn was a consolidation of the Admiralty Court Act 1840, s 6, and the Admiralty Court Act 1861, s 5.

Invoking the jurisdiction of the Admiralty Court

The Admiralty Court's jurisdiction applies to all ships, whether British or not, whether registered or not, wherever the residence of their owners, and in relation to all claims wherever arising.[47] This does not preclude a defendant from arguing that proceedings should be discontinued because the Admiralty Court is not the proper forum according to English rules of private international law. (Later we shall see how arrest nevertheless establishes jurisdiction.)

A claim falling within the jurisdiction of the Admiralty Court can be brought in the Admiralty Court. It might instead be brought in another court, like the Commercial Court. However, pursuant to Civil Procedure Rules r 61.2, the following claims *must* be brought only in the Admiralty Court: a claim *in rem*; for damage done by a ship; concerning the ownership of a ship; under the Merchant Shipping Act 1995; for loss of life or personal injury under s 20(2)(f) of the Senior Courts Act 1981; by a master or member of a crew for wages; in the nature of towage; in the nature of pilotage; a collision claim; a limitation claim; a salvage claim.

---

[47] Senior Courts Act 1981, s 20(7).

Chapter 3 – Claims in rem

When a claimant can sue the ship itself

There are two 'modes of exercise' of admiralty jurisdiction. Claims in the Admiralty Court can be brought *in personam*, that is, against the party who has incurred personal liability, or *in rem*, that is, against property (usually a ship) which has become embroiled in a dispute.[48] The ability to bring a claim *in rem* is a distinctive characteristic of the Admiralty Court. There are two major advantages in bringing a claim *in rem*, at least when the ship is also arrested (we discuss arrest in the next chapter): first, establishing jurisdiction in England; and second, obtaining security (that is, ensuring the successful claimant gets paid).

Any claim that falls within the jurisdiction of the Admiralty Court can be brought *in personam*.[49] Most claims can be brought *in rem*, but not all: a claim for damage received by a ship (that is, claims under s 20(2)(d) of the Senior Courts Act 1981) cannot be brought *in rem*.

Otherwise, there are three types of *in rem* claim. (i) Those against property regardless of ownership (s 21(2) of the Senior Courts Act 1981). (ii) Those against property to which a maritime lien attaches (s 21(3)). (iii) Those against the ship, or a sister ship, where the owner would be liable *in personam* (s 21(4)). We will take each in turn.

---

[48] Service is effected by attaching the claim form to the outside of the ship in a place where it is likely to be seen.

[49] Senior Courts Act 1981, s 21(1).

Claims regardless of ownership (s 21(2))

Claims which can be brought against the property itself, regardless of its owner, are:[50] claims to possession or ownership of a ship (s 20(2)(a)); questions between co-owners as to possession or employment or earnings (s 20(2)(b)); claims in respect of a mortgage or charge on a ship (s 20(2)(c)); claims for forfeiture or condemnation of a ship or goods, or their restoration, or for droits of Admiralty (s 20(2)(s)).

Maritime liens (s 21(3))[51]

Maritime liens are claims upon maritime property which can only be enforced in the Admiralty Court by a claim *in rem*. They arise by operation of law and attach to the property, whether or not the lien holder has possession of the property. They adhere to the property from the time when the facts happened which give rise to the maritime lien.[52] So for example, if a party has provided salvage services to a ship, then they are entitled to be paid, and a maritime lien attaches to the salved ship the moment the services are provided. The lien remains even when the

---

[50] Senior Courts Act 1981, s 21(2).

[51] Senior Courts Act 1981, s 21(3) refers to 'a maritime lien or other charge'. 'Other charge' does not include possessory liens (like a repairer's lien), but does include charges recognised by domestic legislation, as per *The St Merriel* [1963] P 247, or charges under foreign law to secure claims but only if equivalent to those in English law which give rise to a maritime lien, as per *The Acrux* [1965] P 391, 402-403.

[52] *The Two Ellens* (1872) LR 4 PC 161, 169.

property is bought by someone new, even if bought by a good faith purchaser for value without notice.[53]

The ways in which maritime liens are discharged include the total destruction of the property, or its sale by the Admiralty Marshal – the new owner takes free of the maritime lien, but the maritime lien instead now attaches to the proceeds of sale.[54] Maritime liens are also discharged due to laches, that is, the inequitable delay of the lien holder, or when the claim they secure is paid.[55] But an unsatisfied judgment or arbitration award is not enough,[56] nor does the taking of inadequate security necessarily discharge it.[57]

Maritime liens have been recognised for: damage done by a ship as a result of a wrongful act or manoeuvre on its part (for example, through collision);[58] salvage;[59] seamen's wages;[60] and bottomry. Pursuant to statute, there is also a maritime lien for a master's remuneration and disbursements.[61] To the extent that statute provides, in relation to wreck, that the fees and expenses of the receiver,

---

[53] *The Bold Buccleugh* (1851) 7 Moo 267, 13 ER 884 (PC).

[54] *The Sanko Mineral* [2014] EWHC 3927 (Adm), [2015] 1 Lloyd's Rep 247, [41].

[55] If payment is made by a third party, the third party can be subrogated to the position of the lien holder, but only where this happens with the permission of the court.

[56] *The Goulandris* [1927] P 182.

[57] *The Ruta* [2000] 1 WLR 2068 (Adm).

[58] *Currie v M'Knight* [1897] AC 97 (HL). This maritime lien appears to correspond in extent to s 20(2)(e) of the Senior Courts Act 1981.

[59] *The Two Friends* (1799) 165 ER 174, 1 C Rob 271, 277.

[60] *The Sydney Cove* (1815) 2 Dods 11, 165 ER 1399; *The Nymph* (1856) Swa 86, 166 ER 1033.

[61] Merchant Shipping Act 1995, s 41. Disbursements must be made on account of owners, not charterers: *The Castlegate* [1893] AC 38 (HL).

and the remuneration of the coastguard, are recoverable with the same rights as a salvor, by implication that too might create a maritime lien.[62]

Claims under s 21(4)

Claims *in rem* under s 21(4) of the Senior Courts Act 1981, which depend on the personal liability of the defendant, can be brought in the following cases: damage done by a ship (s 20(2)(e)); loss of life or personal injury (s 20(2)(f)); loss of or damage to goods carried in a ship (s 20(2)(g)); claims arising out of any agreement relating to the carriage of goods in a ship, or the use or hire of a ship (s 20(2)(h)); claims in the nature of salvage (s 20(2)(j)); or towage (s 20(2)(k)); or pilotage (s 20(2)(l)); claims in respect of goods or materials supplied to a ship for its operation or maintenance (s 20(2)(m)); claims in respect of the construction, repair or equipment of a ship, or dock charges (s 20(2)(n)); any claim by a master or crew member for wages (s 20(2)(o)); claims by a master, shipper, charterer or agent in respect of disbursements made on account of the ship (s 20(2)(p)); claims arising out of a general average act (s 20(2)(q)); or bottomry (s 20(2)(r)).

Additionally, to bring such a claim: it must arise in connection with a ship; when the cause of action arose, the defendant who would be liable *in personam* was the (registered)[63] owner, or charterer, or person in possession or control of that ship; and when the claim is brought, that defendant must be (a) the

---

[62] Merchant Shipping Act 1995, ss 249(3), 250(3).

[63] *The Evpo Agnic* [1988] 1 WLR 1090 (CA).

34

beneficial owner of all shares in that ship, or its charterer by demise,[64] or (b) the beneficial owner of all shares in the sister ship proceeded against.

In other words, there must be alignment between: the *registered* owner etc at the time when the cause of action arose; and the *beneficial* owner etc at the time when the claim is brought. The purpose of this wording is to prevent an owner who incurs liability from installing a different entity as a fake owner of the ship. If that were allowed: the original owner would have no assets, and so any claim against them would be worthless for being unenforceable; meanwhile, since the new owner is really a fake, the original owner still gets to keep the ship as its beneficial owner.

To put the matter from a different perspective, *in rem* claims under s 21(4) do not survive a genuine change of ownership. They do survive sham changes of ownership. Once the claim form is issued, the claim crystallises and cannot be defeated by a subsequent change in ownership.[65]

The *beneficial* owner is the equitable owner.[66] In identifying the equitable owner, the court can look beyond the registered owner, for example if the registered owner is a trustee or nominee holding.[67] However, most ships are owned by companies, usually 'one-ship' companies whose only asset is a single ship.

---

[64] A ship owner usually retains possession or control of the ship through the (owner's) crew. A charterer usually hires the ship and crew from the owner. A demise charterer (also known as a bareboat charterer or disponent owner) hires the ship alone and supplies its own crew, thus taking full possession and control of the ship.

[65] *The Monica S* [1967] 2 Lloyd's Rep 113 (Adm).

[66] *The I Congreso del Partido* [1978] QB 500 (Adm).

[67] *The Aventicum* [1978] 1 Lloyd's Rep 184 (Adm).

Unless there is fraud, the court will not lift the corporate veil to explore who might be the owner of the company (rather than just the owner of the ship). Shareholders might own a company, but they do not own the company's assets. The company is a legal person, and it alone owns its assets. So for example, even where there are a number of separate one-ship companies, which companies nevertheless have the same officers and shareholders, and whose ships are operated together as part of a fleet, still they are not sister ships for the purposes of s 21(4) of the Senior Courts Act 1981, because the companies which own those ships are different entities one from another.[68]

Note that some of the *in rem* claims which can be brought under s 21(4) overlap with maritime liens. Recall these differences: a maritime lien attaches only to the wrong-doer ship, whereas *in rem* claims under s 21(4) might also be brought against a sister ship; maritime liens remain despite a genuine change in ownership, whereas a genuine change in ownership can preclude an *in rem* claim under s 21(4).

Nature of an *in rem* claim

There is debate as to the precise juridical nature of an *in rem* claim. Is it a claim against the ship itself, or is it really a claim against the ship owner? Is it a procedural technique for bringing a claim, or does it have its own substantive

---

[68] *The Maritime Trader* [1981] 2 Lloyd's Rep 153 (Adm); *The Evpo Agnic* [1988] 1 WLR 1090 (CA).

characteristics? Depending on the answer, there can be consequences. The following pragmatic points are worth noting:

- To repeat, some *in rem* claims can be brought against the ship regardless of whether or not the ship owner has incurred personal liability.

- If an owner does not enter an appearance, then they incur no personal liability.[69] (Of course, they might lose the property.) However, where the owner does enter an appearance, the claim now proceeds *in personam*, and the owner renders themselves open to personal liability.[70]

- Claims *in rem* are said to 'implead' the ship owner, meaning that the ship owner usually has an interest in attending court to defend the property. Indeed, the defendant in an *in rem* claim is usually described in the style 'The Owners of Ship X'.[71] As a result, an *in rem* claim cannot be brought against a ship whose owner enjoys sovereign immunity[72] – unless the ship was used for commercial purposes.[73] (Nor can an *in rem* claim be brought against the Crown.[74]) However, it might be that other defences personal to a ship owner are unavailable when the claim is brought *in rem*.[75]

---

[69] *The Burns* [1907] P 137 (CA), 149.

[70] *The Gemma* [1899] P 285 (CA).

[71] CPR PD 61.3.3.

[72] *The Parlement Belge* (1880) 5 PD 197 (CA); *The Cristina* [1938] AC 485 (HL).

[73] State Immunity Act 1978, s 10.

[74] Crown Proceedings Act 1947, s 29(1); Senior Courts Act 1981, s 24(2)(c).

[75] *The Longford* (1889) 14 PD 34 (CA); *The Burns* [1907] P 137 (CA).

- Importantly, *in rem* claims can have the effect of turning the claimant into a secured creditor, thereby giving it an improved status should the defendant suffer insolvency. This is true with maritime liens, and with other *in rem* claims once issued.[76]

- If a claimant has brought an *in personam* claim against the ship owner, that might preclude a subsequent claim *in rem* on the basis of *res judicata*.[77]

- Whether the facts give rise to a maritime lien is a matter for the *lex fori* (the law governing the hearing of the dispute) and not the *lex causae* (the law governing the substance of the dispute).[78] So just because a foreign law recognises these facts as giving rise to a maritime lien, it does not follow that the Admiralty Court will also recognise it as a maritime lien.

---

[76] *In re Aro Co Ltd* [1980] Ch 196 (CA).

[77] *The Indian Grace (No 2)* [1998] AC 878 (HL).

[78] *The Halcyon Isle* [1981] AC 221 (PC).

Chapter 4 – Arrest

When a ship can be arrested and sold

A claimant or judgment creditor in an *in rem* claim can apply to have the property arrested.[79] So the usual pathology is also follows. Do the facts of the case fall within one of the subject-matter heads of jurisdiction of the Admiralty Court? If so, can the claim be brought *in rem*? If so, an *in rem* claim can be issued, and an application made for a warrant of arrest. An application which complies with the relevant rules leads to the issue of an arrest warrant as of right.[80]

A ship can also be arrested in support of foreign proceedings,[81] and in support of arbitration proceedings.[82] It may be necessary to give notice to the relevant consul if the ship is owned by a state.[83]

Property can only be arrested by the Admiralty Marshal or their substitute.[84] The latter usually means the local officer for UK Borders Agency. The warrant of arrest is executed in the same way as service of an *in rem* claim form,[85] for example by fixing a copy on the outside of the property to be arrested in a position which may reasonably be expected to be seen.[86] For any claim under

---

[79] CPR r 61.5(1).

[80] CPR PD 61.5.2.

[81] Arrest Convention 1952, art 7; Civil Jurisdiction and Judgments Act 1982, s 26.

[82] Arrest Convention 1952, art 7; Arbitration Act 1996, s 11; *Harms Bergung Co v Harms Offshore Co* [2015] EWHC 1269 (Adm).

[83] CPR r 61.5(5).

[84] CPR r 61.5(8).

[85] CPR PD 61.5.5.

s 20(2)(e)-(r) of the Senior Courts Act 1981, only one ship may be served with an *in rem* claim form or arrested.[87] In other words, a claimant cannot arrest multiple ships to enforce one claim. Property under arrest may not be moved unless the court orders otherwise,[88] and anyone who disobeys risks being in contempt of court.

There are two major advantages to arresting a ship: jurisdiction, and security.

Founding jurisdiction

In broad terms, in English law, a claimant can bring an *in personam* claim against a defendant as of right if the defendant can be served with proceedings inside the jurisdiction. If the defendant is outside the jurisdiction, then the claimant may need the permission of the court. An *in rem* claim can only be served inside the jurisdiction.[89] Nevertheless, this does mean that if the ship visits an English port, proceedings can be served as of right on the ship, even if the ship owner is domiciled abroad. However, even where a defendant or ship has been served inside the jurisdiction, or the court has given permission to serve outside the jurisdiction, nevertheless a defendant can still argue that proceedings should not

---

[86] CPR PD 61.3.6(1).

[87] Senior Courts Act 1981, s 21(8).

[88] CPR r 61.5(9).

[89] *The Freccia del Nord* [1989] 1 Lloyd's Rep 388 (Adm).

continue because England is not the proper jurisdiction,[90] according to the English rules of private international law.

The Brussels I Regulation[91] is currently[92] part of the English rules of private international law. In summary, it provides as follows.

It applies in civil and commercial matters (art 1). It does not apply to arbitration (art 2(d)). Its default rules are as follows. Whatever their nationality, persons domiciled in a Member State shall be sued in that Member State (art 4). If the person is not domiciled in a Member State, then domestic rules of private international law will determine jurisdiction (art 6). Both these default principles are subject to exceptions, including the following, whereupon the defendant might be sued in another Member State. In contract, a person may be sued in the courts of the place of performance of the obligation in question (art 7(1)). In tort, a person may be sued in the courts of the place where the harmful event happened (art 7(2)). In a dispute about payment for salvage of cargo or freight, a person may be sued in the courts under whose authority the cargo or freight was arrested, or could have been had security not been given (art 7(7)). The parties can agree jurisdiction in writing (art 25). A court has jurisdiction where a party enters an appearance (other than to contest jurisdiction) (art 26). A Member State party to a

---

[90] A defendant who files an acknowledgment of service to an *in rem* claim does not lose any right to dispute the jurisdiction of the court: CPR PD 61.3.11.

[91] No 1215/2012.

[92] It is an EU law which is directly applicable, and so part of domestic law. After Brexit, the position seems to be that pre-existing EU-derived law which is part of domestic law will continue to be part of domestic law until later addressed – but the political situation is fluid.

convention may apply the jurisdiction rules of that convention, even if the defendant is domiciled in another Member State not party to that convention (art 71).

One such convention[93] is the Arrest Convention 1952,[94] which provides that the arrest of a ship establishes jurisdiction in the country of arrest.[95]

So the short of it is this: if a claim *in rem* is brought in the Admiralty Court against a ship, then the ship can be arrested, and if arrested in England,[96] and served with proceedings, that tends to establish jurisdiction for the Admiralty Court to hear that claim, even if the ship owner or other relevant defendants are domiciled abroad.

---

[93] There are other maritime conventions which might also serve to establish jurisdiction in England, including the Collision Convention 1952, and the Athens Convention 2002 (on injury to passengers).

[94] The UK is party to the Arrest Convention. The provisions of the Arrest Convention have been given effect in English law to the extent that they are reproduced or covered by the Senior Courts Act 1981, ss 20-21, and Pt 61 of the Civil Procedure Rules.

[95] What if the Arrest Convention gives jurisdiction to country A, but a jurisdiction agreement gives jurisdiction to country B? See: *The Maciej Rataj* [1995] 1 Lloyd's Rep 302 (ECJ); *The Bergen* [1997] 1 Lloyd's Rep 380 (Adm); *The Bergen (No 2)* [1997] 2 Lloyd's Rep 710 (Adm).

[96] To invoke the Arrest Convention, the ship must be arrested. It is not enough to accept security from the ship owner in lieu of arrest without the ship owner also agreeing to submit to the jurisdiction: *The Deichland* [1990] 1 QB 361 (CA).

Obtaining security

As for security, when a claim is brought *in rem*, and the ship arrested, if the ship owner does not attend court, then the claimant can seek to make out their claim,[97] and if successful, the ship can be sold,[98] and the proceeds used to meet the judgment. The sale is conducted by the Admiralty Marshal, who can give clean title to the purchaser. If the ship owner does attend court to contest proceedings, usually security will be provided in return for release of the ship, otherwise the ship remains arrested and can be sold. This security is often provided by the ship owner's P&I Club (Protection and Indemnity Club, a group of ship owners who mutually insure). A ship can be re-arrested if further security is required, up to the value of the property.[99]

In ordinary *in personam* proceedings, it can be possible to obtain a freezing injunction to ensure the defendant's assets remain within the jurisdiction pending trial. Arrest is better than a freezing injunction. A freezing injunction merely preserves the asset without giving the claimant any priority to the asset should the defendant become insolvent, whereas an *in rem* claim can convert the claimant into a secured creditor.[100] A cross-undertaking in damages must be given when applying for a freezing injunction, but there is no such requirement with

---

[97] Judgment in default of acknowledgment of service or defence still requires evidence proving the claim: CPR r 61.9(3).

[98] The Admiralty Court has power to sell a ship: Senior Courts Act 1981, s 20(4).

[99] CPR r 61.6.

[100] *The Cella* (1888) 13 PD 82 (CA); *In re Aro Co Ltd* [1980] Ch 196 (CA).

arrest,[101] which instead has the doctrine of wrongful arrest (discussed below), which itself is more generous to the claimant.

Any party who has an interest in the property arrested can apply to be made a party to the claim.[102] They can even defend the claim, but they can only raise defences which the owner could themselves raise.[103]

Wrongful arrest

A defendant may seek damages for wrongful arrest. These are only available where the claimant has acted in *mala fides* (bad faith) or with *crassa negligentia* (crass or gross or 'malicious' negligence).[104] Bad faith tends to mean that the claimant had no honest belief in the entitlement to arrest. Gross negligence tends to mean that there is so little basis for the arrest that it is inferred that the claimant did not believe in the entitlement to arrest or acted without any serious regard as to whether there were adequate grounds for the arrest. A genuine mistake, even an absence of reasonable care, is not enough to amount to gross negligence.[105]

Wrongful arrest was made out in *Gulf Azov Shipping Co Ltd v Idisi*.[106] There the ship was arrested to support a claim for a hugely inflated sum for which

---

[101] *The MV Alkyon* [2018] EWCA Civ 2760.

[102] CPR r 61.8(7).

[103] *The Byzantion* (1922) 12 Ll L Rep 9 (Adm), 11-12.

[104] *The Evangelismos* (1858) 12 Moo 352 (PC), 14 ER 945; *The Strathnaver* (1875) 1 App Cas 58 (PC).

[105] *The Kommunar (No 3)* [1997] 1 Lloyd's Rep 22 (Adm), 30.

[106] [2001] EWCA Civ 491, [2001] 1 Lloyd's Rep 727.

there was no objective justification as the arresting party must have known perfectly well. The arrest was prolonged, on an improper basis for an unconscionable period of time, and involved the detention of the whole crew, when at best only a skeleton crew was needed. Damages for wrongful arrest were payable.

It may also amount to wrongful arrest to continue for too long what was originally an acceptable arrest. For example, in *The Cheshire Witch*,[107] the claimant considered appealing an adverse decision, but ultimately decided not to, yet persisted with the arrest during that 12 day period of reflection. Damages were payable for that period. In *The Margaret Jane*,[108] the claimant brought proceedings in the Admiralty Court, seeking to recover more money than the valuation declared by the receiver of wreck. It soon became apparent that the receiver's valuation was broadly correct, so damages were awarded for persisting with the arrest thereafter.

Additionally, a party may file a caution against arrest, which is then entered into the register kept for that purpose at the Admiralty and Commercial Registry.[109] A search of this register must be made before making an application for arrest.[110] The party requesting the caution undertakes to the court to acknowledge service and give sufficient security to satisfy the claim with interest and costs.[111] Any *in rem* claim form is then served on the person named in the

---

[107] (1864) Br & L 362.

[108] (1869) LR 2 Ad & E 345.

[109] CPR r 61.7; CPR PD 61.6.3.

[110] CPR r 61.5(3).

47

caution as being entitled to accept service.[112] (This is not treated as submission to the jurisdiction.[113]) Thereafter the ship might remain free. However, property might still be arrested if there is a good and sufficient reason.[114] But otherwise, where arrest is made despite the caution, the court can order the arresting party to pay compensation (separately from the doctrine of wrongful arrest).[115]

In *The Crimdon*,[116] a caution against arrest was accompanied by an undertaking given by solicitors, which rendered them personally liable. Instead of investigating the sufficiency of that security, as they should have done, the claimant arrested the ship for security instead. That was not a good reason for arrest, and damages were payable.

---

[111] CPR r 61.7(2).

[112] CPR PD 61.3.6(4).

[113] CPR PD 61.6.1.

[114] Arrest to establish jurisdiction ought to be a good reason.

[115] CPR r 61.7(5).

[116] [1900] P 171.

Release from arrest

A ship under arrest can be arrested by any other party with an *in rem* claim against it.[117] More usual is to file a caution against release, also entered in the register,[118] which entitles them to notice of any application in respect of the property.[119]

A ship will be released from arrest in a number of cases, including where the arresting party and all those with cautions against release agree.[120] Any delay to the release caused by the entry of a caution against release might sound in damages,[121] for example where objection to the release was groundless,[122] unless there was good reason to maintain the caution.[123] Usually the court will order release only where the defendant has provided sufficient security to cover the amount of the claim plus interest and costs, on the basis of the claimant's best reasonably arguable case.[124] A claimant cannot ask for greater security than the value of the property arrested. If the parties cannot agree the value of the property arrested, the court can make an order for appraisement.

---

[117] CPR r 61.8(1).

[118] CPR PD 61.7.2.

[119] CPR r 61.8(2). However, it may be necessary to issue an *in rem* claim form in order to crystallize rights, or to arrest the ship in order to establish jurisdiction.

[120] CPR r 61.8(4).

[121] CPR r 61.8(5).

[122] *The Don Ricardo* (1880) 5 PD 121.

[123] CPR r 61.8(6).

[124] *The Moschanthy* [1971] 1 Lloyd's Rep 37 (Adm); *The Tribels* [1985] 1 Lloyd's Rep 128 (Adm).

Sale of the ship

After trial, the ship may be sold to satisfy the judgment, in the absence of any other security. A ship can also be sold pending trial. Such a course of action will not be taken except for good reason, a question the court will examine critically. A good reason can include the heavy and continuing costs of maintaining an arrest incurred over a long period with subsequent diminution of the funds available to meet the claim (and to protect any residual financial interest in the ship by its owners).[125]

Usually the value of the ship is appraised, unless for example its value seems slight and the costs of appraisement would severely eat into the sale proceeds. The ship is then sold by the Admiralty Marshal, either for the best price obtainable, or if appraised, for not less than the appraised value (unless the court gives permission). The Admiralty Marshal might incur costs in order to achieve a better sale price, for example by repairs, or repatriating the crew. An owner can try to sell a ship under arrest, assuming anyone would risk buying it, but once an order has been made by the court for sale by the Admiralty Marshal, any attempt by the owner to sell the ship privately amounts to contempt for hindering the work of the Admiralty Marshal.[126]

When a ship is sold by the Admiralty Marshal, the purchaser takes it free of any maritime liens or any other maritime claims.[127] Pre-existing *in rem* claims

---

[125] *The Myrto* [1977] 2 Lloyd's Rep 243 (Adm), 260.

[126] *The Jarvis Brake* [1976] 2 Lloyd's Rep 320 (Adm).

[127] *The Cerro Colorado* [1995] 1 Lloyd's Rep 58 (Adm).

can instead be made against the proceeds of sale in the hands of the court.[128] Service is effected by filing the claim form at court.[129]

Priorities

If the proceeds of sale are insufficient to meet all claims, and the parties cannot reach agreement on the distribution of the fund, then the court will need to determine priorities. Any party with a judgment against the property or its proceeds may apply to the court for determination of priorities, giving notice to anyone who has filed a claim against the property, in order to obtain payment out of the proceeds of sale.[130]

The court exercises an equitable jurisdiction to determine the order of priorities from case to case as justice requires. This is an area which can get technical, giving rise to nice questions of law. But in overall shape the position is clear enough, and the court tends to follow a settled practice unless justice requires a departure in a particular case. That settled practice is broadly as follows.

First, the Admiralty Court gives precedence to a body with a statutory power of detention and sale, if that power is exercised.[131] An example of such a power is one accorded to a harbour authority to recover tonnage rates.[132]

---

[128] *The Sanko Mineral* [2014] EWHC 3927 (Adm), [2015] 1 Lloyd's Rep 247, [41].

[129] CPR PD 61.3.6(3).

[130] CPR r 61.10(3).

[131] *The Charger* [1966] 1 Lloyd's Rep 670 (Adm).

[132] Harbours Docks and Piers Clauses Act 1847, s 44.

Next priority goes to the Admiralty Marshal's charges and expenses,[133] then the costs (not claims) of the original arresting party, and the costs of the party obtaining appraisement and sale, since these costs were incurred to produce the fund for the benefit of all creditors.[134]

As for substantive claims, maritime liens rank first. Maritime liens of the same type rank equally, except that later salvage ranks ahead of earlier salvage, because it preserved the property.[135] With maritime liens of different types, the order is generally: priority to the last person to preserve the property; wages; damage done by the ship.

The holder of a common law possessory lien tends to have priority over all other claims except for pre-existing maritime liens.[136] An example of a common law possessory lien is repair work carried out on a ship. Mortgages rank next, then *in rem* claims granted by statute (rather than based upon a maritime lien).

Any leftover proceeds are paid to the owner of the property – whose finances might be further diminished by *in personam* claims against them. Thus it is worth emphasising that priorities are concerned with selling the property, and who gets a share of that money. *In personam* claimants have no interest in the property. They can only sue its owner.

---

[133] When filing an application for arrest, a party must undertake to pay all expenses and fees incurred by the Admiralty Marshal: CPR PD 61.5.1.

[134] *The Rana* (1921) 8 Ll L Rep 369 (Adm); *The Athena* (1921) 8 Ll L Rep 482 (Adm).

[135] *The Lyrma (No 2)* [1978] 2 Lloyd's Rep 30 (Adm), 34.

[136] *The Gustaf* (1862) Lush 506, 167 ER 230.

A case study in priorities is provided by *The Ruta*.[137] A cargo ship collided with three moored yachts. Claims were brought by the mortgagees and the unpaid crew. The court articulated its reasoning on priorities as follows. No-one could claim to have preserved the property, so no priority arose on that basis. Protecting mariners is a high priority for the Admiralty Court, whereas prioritising damage claims as an indirect mechanism to increase careful navigation was 'somewhat quaint' as a justification. The damage here was not caused by crew negligence, which might have reduced their priority. The clinching factor was that the wage claimants had no other form of redress, and their claim was likely to be smaller than a claim for damage, leaving some funds left over for the damage claimants, when the latter might have exhausted the whole fund had they been given priority.

---

[137] [2000] 1 WLR 2068 (QBD).

Chapter 5 – Limitation

Time limits, and limits to the amount of compensation

'Limitation' can mean two things. It can mean that there is a limited time within which to bring a claim. Or it can mean that the defendant can limit their liability, in other words, that there is a limited amount of compensation which a defendant has to pay if they are found liable. We shall take each in turn.

Time limits

Normally, under the Limitation Act 1980, claims in contract and tort must be brought within 6 years, and claims for personal injury within 3 years. However, maritime law provides for a range of different time limits, including the following.

Under the York-Antwerp Rules, claims for a general average contribution must be brought within one year.

The Hague-Visby Rules tend to govern carriage of goods by ship.[138] Claims must be brought within one year of the date when the cargo was or should have been delivered, although the parties may agree an extension after the cause of action has arisen.[139] It is a substantive time bar which extinguishes the claim or counterclaim or set-off (rather than merely barring the remedy),[140] though it need not preclude a *defence*.[141]

---

[138] Enacted through the Carriage of Goods by Sea Act 1971. The Hague-Visby Rules are an amended version of their predecessor, the Hague Rules, which also have a one year time limit.

[139] Hague-Visby Rules, Art III r 6.

A less common alternative regime for bills of lading is the Hamburg Rules, which have a two year time limit.

A claim between owners and time charterers under a time charter party on the New York Produce Exchange standard form, which incorporates the Inter-Club New York Produce Exchange Agreement, concerning the allocation of liability for cargo claims, provides that written notification of such a claim must be given within 24 months of when the cargo was or should have been delivered, or 36 months if the Hamburg Rules apply.

Under the Merchant Shipping Act 1995, there is a two year time limit for the following claims: damage caused, by the fault of the defendant ship, to the claimant ship or its cargo or freight or property on board; loss of life or personal injury, caused by the fault of the defendant ship, to any person on board another ship.[142] So this does not cover, for example, claims for personal injury suffered by those on board the defendant ship, or for damage to cargo carried on board the defendant ship. In other words, this section always requires two different ships. The court has discretion to extend the time limit,[143] and shall do so where there has not yet been a reasonable opportunity for arrest.[144]

The Athens Convention 2002, concerning claims by passengers for personal injury or loss of luggage, has a two year time limit.

---

[140] *The Aries* [1977] 1 WLR 185 (HL), 188.

[141] *The Fiona* [1994] 2 Lloyd's Rep 506 (CA).

[142] Merchant Shipping Act 1995, s 190.

[143] Merchant Shipping Act 1995, s 190(5).

[144] Merchant Shipping Act 1995, s 190(6).

Claims under the Salvage Convention must also be brought within two years.

Limitation of liability

Historically, the potential for a ship owner to limit their liability in English law originated in a statute of 1734.[145] It allowed a ship owner to limit their liability, to the value of the ship plus freight, for loss of gold, silver, diamonds, jewels, precious stones, and other goods and merchandise, stolen by the crew without the privity or knowledge of the ship owner.[146] The preamble to the statute gave the following rationale. It would discourage merchants from 'adventuring their fortunes' as ship owners if they were to be liable for what happened on board without their knowledge. This in turn would reduce the number of ships, and so the volume of trade and navigation, to the detriment of the kingdom.

Over time, statutory law developed to allow a ship owner to limit their liability, to a sum based on the tonnage of the ship, against any claim for which they were not personally at fault. This became the basis of three international conventions, all variations on a theme, the most ratified being the Convention on Limitation of Liability for Maritime Claims 1976 ('the Limitation Convention'). This is enacted into English law with variations by the Merchant Shipping Act

---

[145] 7 Geo 2 c 15.

[146] If the limited compensation was insufficient, cargo owners could 'receive their Satisfaction thereout in Average'.

1995.[147] The limit of liability was increased by the 1996 Protocol, and raised again in 2012.[148]

Who can limit. By article 1 of the Limitation Convention, the ability to limit applies to the ship owner, insurer, charterer,[149] manager, operator, salvor, and any person for whom these others are responsible.

When limitation available. By article 2, the types of claims which can be limited include the following: loss of life or personal injury, or loss of or damage to property, occurring on board or in direct connection with the operations of the ship, or with salvage operations, and consequential loss resulting therefrom; and delay in the carriage by sea. 'Damage to property' is not restricted to physical damage, but can include diminution in value, for example due to delay or a salvage lien.[150] Note that damage to the ship itself is not within the limitation regime.[151]

By article 3, limitation is not available for claims including the following:[152] salvage; general average; personal injury, or damage to the property, of persons on

---

[147] Merchant Shipping Act 1995, s 185, and sch 7.

[148] Merchant Shipping Act 1995 (Amendment) Order 2016 (SI 2016 No 1061).

[149] Including slot charterer: *The MSC Napoli* [2009] 1 Lloyd's Rep 246 (Adm).

[150] *The Breydon Merchant* [1992] 1 Lloyd's Rep 373 (Adm).

[151] *The CMA Djakarta* [2004] EWCA Civ 114; *The Ocean Victory* [2017] UKSC 35.

[152] Note also that there are different regimes under the Oil Pollution Convention 1969 (oil pollution by oil tankers), and for damage involving nuclear material, and for hazardous material, and in respect of harbour authorities and dock and canal owners, and for pilotage.

board under a contract of service governed by English law.[153] Note that while a direct claim against the ship owner for their personal contribution for salvage or general average cannot be limited, a claim by cargo owners against the ship owner for an indemnity to cover their (cargo owner's) salvage or general average contributions can be limited.[154]

Liability can be limited for all claims 'arising on any distinct occasion'.[155] This means that no matter how many claims arise, if they all arise on one occasion, then a global limit of liability is applied to all claims cumulatively, and on behalf of all possible defendants.[156] The corollary is that if claims arise on separate occasions, then the limit of liability starts again for each occasion. So for example, two collisions on the same voyage, even if close in time, will be two separate occasions if the second could have been independently avoided, and when the first was no cause of the second.[157] But where a single act of negligent seamanship caused a ship to collide with two others at the same time,[158] or the first collision was the substantial and efficacious cause of the second,[159] then there is only one occasion.

---

[153] See: Merchant Shipping Act 1995, s 185(4).

[154] *The Breydon Merchant* [1992] 1 Lloyd's Rep 373 (Adm); *The Aegean Sea* [1998] 2 Lloyd's Rep 39 (Adm), 55.

[155] Limitation Convention, art 6.

[156] Limitation Convention, art 9, art 11(3).

[157] *The Schwan* [1892] P 419 (CA).

[158] *The Rajah* (1872) LR 3 A & E 539 (Adm).

[159] *The Creadon* (1886) 54 LT 880 (Adm).

Loss of right to limit. It is possible to contract out of the right to limit.[160] Also, by article 4, the right to limit can be lost if the loss resulted from a personal act or omission, committed with intent to cause such loss, or recklessly and with knowledge that 'such loss'[161] would probably result. For example, where the master and chief engineer deliberately set fire to and sank the ship on the orders of the director of the ship owning company, thereby damaging cargo, that forfeited the right to limit.[162]

Amount of limit. The limit is a number of Special Drawing Rights (SDRs),[163] which increases according to the tonnage of the ship.[164] (SDR is the unit of account of the International Monetary Fund, whose value is determined by a basket of currencies.) There is a higher limit for personal injury claims, and a lower limit for all other claims.[165] The exception is personal injury to *passengers* on board non-sea-going ships, when the limit depends, not on tonnage, but on the number of passengers which the ship is certificated to carry.[166] (For passengers on sea-going ships, the limits in the Athens Convention 2002 apply.)[167]

---

[160] *The Cape Bari* [2016] 2 Lloyd's Rep 469 (PC).

[161] This means the very loss which actually occurred, and not merely generic 'damage to property': *The Leerort* [2001] EWCA Civ 1055, [2001] 2 Lloyd's Rep 291.

[162] *The Atlantik Confidence* [2016] EWHC 2412 (Adm), [2016] 2 Lloyd's Rep 525.

[163] Limitation Convention, art 8.

[164] Limitation Convention, art 6.

[165] If the fund for personal injury is not sufficient to meet all personal injury claims, any balance can be drawn from the fund for property damage, where personal injury claims will rank rateably: Limitation Convention, art 6(2).

Procedure. The right to limit liability can be pleaded as a defence,[168] but this approach is only binding on the parties to that litigation. To bind all possible claimants, the ship owner should initiate a claim (or counterclaim),[169] seeking a general limitation decree. Once a decree is given, it is advertised,[170] so that claimants can come forward. Their claims are served on the ship owner and all other claimants,[171] since the latter have an interest in ensuring that the limited compensation is paid out only to deserving claimants.

It is not necessary to constitute a limitation fund,[172] for example, by paying money into court or providing security,[173] rather than just seeking a declaration of the right to limit.[174] But if a fund is constituted, then a claimant cannot exercise rights against the ship owner's assets.[175] For example, they cannot arrest the ship, and a ship owner can enter a caution against arrest.[176] Once the

---

[166] Limitation Convention, art 7.

[167] See Merchant Shipping Act 1995, sch 7, Pt II, para 2(A), para 6.

[168] CPR PD 61.10.18.

[169] In form ADM15: CPR PD 61.11.1. Counterclaims for a general limitation decree require the permission of the court: CPR r 61.11(22). Limitation claims must be brought in the Admiralty Court: CPR r 61.2(1)(c).

[170] CPR r 61.11(14).

[171] CPR r 61.11(15).

[172] CPR r 61.11(19).

[173] CPR r 61.11(18).

[174] Although the court may order a fund to be constituted once a limitation decree is granted: CPR r 61.11(13).

[175] Limitation Convention, art 13(1).

[176] CPR r 61.7.2(b).

fund is constituted, any ship arrested can be released.[177] The fund is distributed among the claimants in proportion to the relative values of their proven claims.[178] (There are no 'priorities' for a limitation fund.)[179] Costs are outside the limitation regime.

Jurisdiction. The question of jurisdiction is somewhat muddled, because the Limitation Convention does not say exhaustively when a court can entertain a limitation plea. In overview, the position seems to be that if the ship owner is a defendant, then they can plead limitation in that action.[180] If the ship owner wants to be pro-active and seek a limitation decree before claims are made against them, then this can be done in any state party to the Limitation Convention whose courts have personal jurisdiction over the would-be claimants.[181] If would-be claimants are EU domiciled, a decree can be sought in the state where the would-be claimants are domiciled,[182] or perhaps also in the EU state where the ship owner is domiciled.[183] Presumably a limitation decree can also be sought in a jurisdiction to

---

[177] Property *must* be released, if the limitation fund is constituted in one of four places specified in the Limitation Convention, art 13(2).

[178] Limitation Convention, art 12(1).

[179] For example, there is no priority for maritime liens: Merchant Shipping Act 1995, schedule 7, Part II, para 9.

[180] Limitation Convention, art 11(1); *The ICL Vikraman* [2003] EWHC 2320 (Comm).

[181] *The Western Regent* [2005] EWCA Civ 985.

[182] Because technically the would-be claimants against the ship owner then become defendants to the limitation claim, engaging art 4 of the Brussels I Regulation (No 1215/2012).

[183] Under art 9 of the Brussels I Regulation, on the basis that the ship owner would have to be sued in

which the parties have agreed to submit, or have submitted, or which is otherwise seised of the matter. For non-EU parties, English domestic law applies, and the Admiralty Court has jurisdiction by virtue of the Senior Courts Act 1981.[184]

Total exclusions. In addition to limiting liability, there is also a total exclusion of liability in respect of a United Kingdom ship:[185] for loss or damage to property on board caused by fire,[186] or theft of gold, silver, watches, jewels or precious stones whose nature and value was not declared in the bill of lading. This extends to the owner, charterer, manager, operator, master or crew member. It does not apply (by cross-referencing the Limitation Convention) where the loss or damage results from the personal act or omission of the defendant committed with intent to cause such loss, or recklessly and with knowledge that such loss would probably result.

their EU state of domicile by would-be claimants themselves complying with art 4.

[184] Senior Courts Act 1981, s 20(1)(b). At which point, permission to serve out of the jurisdiction may be needed: CPR r 61.11(5); *The ICL Vikraman* [2003] EWHC 2320 (Comm).

[185] Merchant Shipping Act 1995, s 186.

[186] 'Fire' includes damage caused by smoke, or water used to fight the fire: *The Diamond* [1906] P 282.

Chapter 6 – Salvage

Rewards for saving property at sea

A person who saves property on land is usually entitled to nothing for their efforts. A person who saves property at sea is a salvor, and may be entitled to a salvage award. Salvage also attracts a maritime lien.[187]

Salvage is governed by the International Convention on Salvage 1989 ('the Salvage Convention'), which is given the force of law by the Merchant Shipping Act 1995.[188] Parties are able to contract out of the Salvage Convention.[189] However, much professional salvage is undertaken pursuant to a standard form contract called Lloyd's Standard Form of Salvage Agreement, more commonly called Lloyd's Open Form (LOF).[190] This provides for London arbitration and English law, and of course English law includes the Salvage Convention.[191] Otherwise, ordinary contract law principles apply to LOF.[192]

---

[187] *The Two Friends* (1799) 1 C Rob 271, 277; 165 ER 174.

[188] Merchant Shipping Act 1995, s 224, and sch 11.

[189] Salvage Convention, art 6.

[190] For a rare example of non-contractual salvage, where the court nevertheless applied the Salvage Convention, see: *The Kuzma Minin* [2019] EWHC 3557 (Adm).

[191] *The Altair* [2008] EWHC 612 (Comm); [2008] 2 Lloyd's Rep 90.

[192] *The Unique Mariner (No 2)* [1979] 1 Lloyd's Rep 37 (Adm).

Salvage contract

Under the Salvage Convention, the master of any ship in danger has authority to conclude a salvage contract on behalf of the owners of the ship; and the master and ship owners (including authorised employees)[193] have authority to conclude a salvage contract on behalf of the owners of any property on board.[194]

Any contract, or its individual terms, can be annulled, or modified, if entered into under undue influence or the influence of danger and its terms are inequitable, or if the payment under the contract is in an excessive degree too large or too small for the services actually rendered.[195] In other words, the salvage contract can be rewritten by the courts.

Salvage services rendered without a contract can be desisted by the salvor or the salvee at any time. If rendered under LOF, there is a contractual duty on salvors to use best endeavours to salve the property. As a corollary, the courts have implied a term not to prevent the salvors from doing so, breach of which might sound in damages.[196] However, LOF expressly allows termination by either party where there is no longer any reasonable prospect of a useful result.

---

[193] *The Altair* [2008] EWHC 612 (Comm), [2008] 2 Lloyd's Rep 90, [42], where it included an employee of the ship's managers.

[194] Salvage Convention, art 6(2).

[195] Salvage Convention, art 7.

[196] *The Unique Mariner (No 2)* [1979] 1 Lloyd's Rep 37 (Adm), where the ship, in breach of contract, purported to dismiss the original salvors and replace them.

66

What can be salved

Under the Salvage Convention, a 'salvage operation' means any act or activity undertaken to assist a vessel or any other property in danger in any waters.[197] However, English domestic law excludes salvage operations in inland waters, when all vessels are of inland navigation, or when no vessel is involved.[198] 'Vessel' means any ship or craft, or any structure capable of navigation.[199] This tends to align with the meaning of 'ship' for ascertaining the jurisdiction of the Admiralty Court. So for example, this excludes salvage rendered to a moored gas float, acting as a lightship, not intended to be navigated.[200] 'Property' means any property not permanently and intentionally attached to the shoreline, and includes freight at risk.[201] LOF excludes personal effects or baggage of passengers or crew (who therefore do not have to contribute to the salvage award).

Traditionally, life salvage went unrewarded, because the 'fund' from which salvage was paid was 'constituted' by the property saved.[202] In other words, salvage could be paid by realising the value of property saved, and of course one cannot sell a person or attach them with a maritime lien. Now, under the Salvage Convention, a salvor of human life is entitled to a fair share of the payment

---

[197] Salvage Convention, art 1(a).

[198] Merchant Shipping Act 1995, sch 11, Pt II, para 2; *The Goring* [1988] AC 831 (HL).

[199] Salvage Convention, art 1(b).

[200] *The Gas Float Whitton No 2* [1897] AC 337 (HL).

[201] Salvage Convention, art 1(c).

[202] *The Repnor* (1883) 8 PD 115 (CA).

awarded to the salvor who saved property or prevented damage to the environment.[203] In English domestic law, a life salvor may also be entitled to payment by the Secretary of State.[204] Additionally, a master of a vessel is obliged to render assistance to any person in danger of being lost at sea, so far as they can do so without serious danger to their ship or the people aboard.[205] Failure to discharge this duty is a criminal offence.[206]

Danger

Only property which is in danger can be salved.[207] There need not be actual or imminent danger, but a state of difficulty, and the reasonable apprehension of danger;[208] it suffices that the ship has encountered damage or misfortune which might possibly expose it to destruction.[209] By 'might' is meant a real, as opposed to fanciful, possibility.[210] Or putting it another way, the question is whether the ship is so exposed to damage that no reasonable person would refuse the salvor's offer of assistance.[211] As for LOF, it expressly provides that 'services shall be

---

[203] Salvage Convention, art 16.

[204] Merchant Shipping Act 1995, sch 11, Pt II, para 5.

[205] Salvage Convention, art 10.

[206] Merchant Shipping Act 1995, sch 11, Pt II, para 3.

[207] This also follows from the definition of salvage operations in the Salvage Convention, art 1(a).

[208] *The Phantom* (1866) LR 1 A & E 58 (Adm), 60.

[209] *The Charlotte* (1848) 3 W Rob 68, 166 ER 888.

[210] *The Mount Cynthos* (1937) 58 Ll L Rep 18 (Adm), 25.

[211] *The Tramp* [2007] EWHC 31 (Adm), [2007] 2 Lloyd's Rep 363.

rendered and accepted as salvage services', and this estopps a salvee from denying that the property was in danger.[212]

Under the Salvage Convention,[213] the offer of salvage may be expressly rejected by the salvee, if reasonable to do so, in which case the salvor is not entitled to any payment. However, if any assistance was reasonably prudent after all, the salvor can seek payment, even if the salvee attempted to reject the assistance.[214]

It follows from the need for danger that there is no further salvage once the property reaches a place of safety. When is a ship safe? In *The Glaucus*,[215] a ship suffered serious damage to her boilers and was unable to steam until repaired. It was towed from the Indian Ocean to anchorage at Aden. But there were no facilities there for repair, so in effect the ship remained beyond use (though we might say that it was temporarily 'safe'). It was towed again to Suez for repairs. Both towages were held to constitute salvage.[216]

---

[212] See *The Kafiristan* [1938] AC 136 (HL), 140, where it was said that the defendant was precluded from denying that services under LOF did indeed amount to salvage.

[213] Salvage Convention, art 19.

[214] *The August Legembre* [1902] P 123.

[215] (1947) 81 Ll L Rep 262 (Adm), 266.

[216] Similarly, see *Troilus v Glenogle* [1951] AC 820 (HL), where the ship was towed first to anchorage at Aden, and then to the UK for repairs, and both towages were held to constitute salvage.

Volunteer

A salvor must have no prior duty to help. For example, the Salvage Convention states that no salvage payment is due unless the services rendered exceed what can be reasonably considered as due performance of any contract entered into before the danger arose.[217] Thus the crew of the ship salved cannot claim salvage, even if they help, because preserving the ship is part of their job – unless their prior duties had been discharged because the master had ordered the ship to be abandoned.[218] So too a contract of towage will not subsequently become salvage unless the tug goes beyond what it was contractually obliged to do.[219] Similarly, owners of the property in danger can claim salvage against the ship only if they act beyond what is ordinarily expected of them.[220]

A ship owner cannot claim for salving their own ship; but they can claim for salving cargo on board (unless the danger was caused by their own breach of contract); and they can claim for salving a sister ship.[221]

---

[217] Salvage Convention, art 17.

[218] *The San Demetrio* (1941) 69 Ll L Rep 5 (Adm).

[219] See *The Aldora* [1975] QB 748 (QBD), where the tug could claim salvage when the tow went aground and needed to be refloated.

[220] *The Sava Star* [1995] 2 Lloyd's Rep 134 (Adm).

[221] *The Sava Star* [1995] 2 Lloyd's Rep 134 (Adm); Salvage Convention, art 12(3).

Success

Under the Salvage Convention, salvage operations which have had a useful result give right to a reward, whereas no payment is due if the salvage operations have had no useful result.[222] In other words, salvage must be successful. This is not so, for example, if the salved property is merely taken from one danger and left in another.[223] Making the point clear, LOF is headed in bold capitals: 'No cure – no pay'.

Duties of care

Art 8 of the Salvage Convention imposes duties of care on both salvor and salvee, including the following. The salvor must act with due care, and seek assistance when reasonably required, and accept assistance when reasonably requested. The salvee must cooperate fully, and accept redelivery at the place of safety. Both must exercise due care to prevent or minimise damage to the environment. Any breach of these duties might result in a counterclaim for damages.

For example, where salvors successfully salved a tanker and its cargo, but by their negligence caused damage to the tanker, the owners of the tanker could counterclaim, even where that produced a net payment to the tanker owners.[224] And where the negligence of the salvee prevented the ship from being rescued, the

---

[222] Salvage Convention, art 12.

[223] *The Melanie* [1925] AC 246 (HL), 262.

[224] *The Tojo Maru* [1972] AC 242 (HL).

salvors, although they had not succeeded in rescuing the ship, were still entitled by way of damages to a sum equivalent to the remuneration they would have earned but for the salvee's negligence.[225]

A salvor may be deprived of the whole or part of their award to the extent that the salvage operations have become necessary or more difficult because of fault or neglect on their part, or if the salvor has been guilty of fraud or other dishonest conduct.[226] Similarly, if a salvor has been negligent and has thereby failed to prevent or minimise damage to the environment, they may be deprived of the whole or part of any 'special compensation' (as to the meaning of which, see below).[227]

Salvage award

The salved property is valued. This is the maximum limit for any award.[228] Each owner contributes to the award in proportion to the value of their property.[229] Each owner is liable only for its share.[230]

Art 13 of the Salvage Convention sets the criteria for fixing the award. The award is fixed expressly with a view to encouraging salvage operations, and

---

[225] *The Valsesia* [1927] P 115 (Adm).

[226] Salvage Convention, art 18.

[227] Salvage Convention, art 14(5).

[228] Salvage Convention, art 13(3).

[229] Salvage Convention, art 13(2).

[230] *The Geestland* [1980] 1 Lloyd's Rep 628 (Adm).

includes the following considerations: the value of salved property, the measure of success, the degree of danger, the skill and effort expended, time and expense incurred, risk of liability, promptness of service, and the state of readiness and efficiency of the salvor's equipment and its value. These criteria also decide the apportionment of the award where several salvors have been involved in the same salvage operations.[231]

Salvage attracts a maritime lien. The salvor may not enforce the maritime lien when satisfactory security for the claim, including interest and costs, has been duly tendered or provided.[232] Upon the request of the salvor, a person liable for payment shall provide satisfactory security for the claim, including interest and costs;[233] and the owner of the salved vessel shall use their best endeavours to ensure that the owners of the cargo provide satisfactory security for the claims against them.[234] Further, the salved vessel and other property shall not, without the consent of the salvor, be removed from the place at which they first arrive after the completion of the salvage operations until satisfactory security has been put up.[235] There is a 2 year time bar for bringing salvage claims.[236]

---

[231] Salvage Convention, art 15.

[232] Salvage Convention, art 20(2).

[233] Salvage Convention, art 21(1).

[234] Salvage Convention, art 21(2).

[235] Salvage Convention, art 21(3).

[236] Salvage Convention, art 23.

LOF provides for arbitration in London with English law, in accordance with the Lloyd's Salvage Arbitration Clauses (LSAC). In turn, LSAC provides that salvors will not arrest property, unless security is not provided.

Environmental damage

By art 14(1) of the Salvage Convention, if a salvor has carried out salvage operations in respect of a ship which, by itself or its cargo, has threatened damage to the environment, then the salvor is entitled to 'special compensation', being the amount of their expenses. This is so where the salvor has failed to earn a reward under art 13 at all (for example, because the ship was not successfully salved), or at least has failed to earn a reward in an equivalent amount. Further, if the salvor has actually prevented or minimised damage to the environment, then they can ask for a discretionary uplift, under art 14(2), of up to 100% on their expenses. This is payable by the ship owner, although their right of recourse (if any) is expressly preserved.[237]

There is also the Special Compensation P&I Club ('SCOPIC') clause, which can be incorporated into LOF. This provides, in place of art 14 of the Salvage Convention, an agreed schedule of prices for different salvage services rendered to protect the environment, with an uplift of up to 25%.

---

[237] Salvage Convention, art 14(6).

Relationship with limitation and general average

Under the Limitation Convention, art 3, claims for salvage, including any claim for special compensation under art 14, are excluded from limitation.[238] That is, claims *for* salvage, by salvors, are excluded from limitation. But not excluded are claims to an indemnity, such as a claim by a cargo owner against the ship owner, requiring the ship owner to provide an indemnity to cover the cargo owner's salvage contribution, on the basis that this contribution was incurred due to the ship owner's breach of charter party (in not providing a seaworthy ship).[239]

The York-Antwerp Rules exclude from general average any award under art 14 or SCOPIC,[240] since these reward activities to protect the environment rather than to protect property imperilled by the common adventure. SCOPIC also expressly excludes itself from general average. Further, the York-Antwerp Rules usually[241] exclude from general average any (ordinary) salvage award when the parties have separate liabilities to the salvor – and indeed, liability is usually several rather than joint.

---

[238] Limitation Convention, art 3.

[239] *The Breydon Merchant* [1992] 1 Lloyd's Rep 373.

[240] York-Antwerp Rules 2016, r VI(d).

[241] Unless an exceptional event occurs from the list in the York-Antwerp Rules 2016, r VI(b).

Chapter 7 – General Average

Sacrifices made for the greater good

General average is usually governed by the York-Antwerp Rules. (References here are to the 2016 Rules.) These do not have independent force of law in England, but they are usually incorporated expressly into the governing contract (such as the charter party or bill of lading). General average can otherwise be available as a matter of common law.

General average is a right to seek a contribution for any extraordinary sacrifice or expenditure, intentionally and reasonably made or incurred for the common safety, for the purpose of preserving from peril the property involved in a common maritime adventure.[242] The parties involved in the common maritime adventure are the ship owner, the cargo owners, and the party entitled to freight.[243] Each party must make a contribution proportionate to the value of their interest or property.[244] This means that the party which made the sacrifice must also bear their own share.

---

[242] York-Antwerp Rules, r A.

[243] Loss of freight is itself allowed as general average when it was payable in respect of cargo which has been lost or damaged, when that damage to cargo was itself the general average act, or when it was caused by another general average act: York-Antwerp Rules, r XV.

[244] York-Antwerp Rules, r XVII. Where cargo is undeclared or wilfully misdescribed, it cannot claim in general average, but must contribute: r XIX(a). Where the value of goods has been wrongfully under-declared, they can claim in general average at their declared value, but must contribute at their actual value: r XIX(b).

For example, A's cargo (worth £100) might be jettisoned in order to save B's ship (worth £700) and C's cargo (worth £200) which remains on board. Their respective shares are 10%, 70%, and 20%. Thus A would have to bear £10 of the loss, but recovers contributions from B and C to the sum of £90. In this way, general average is a form of mutual insurance.

Fault

If the need for a general average act was due to the fault of one party, recourse claims can be made against that party.[245] Similarly, if the need for the general average act was caused by the actionable fault of the claimant, that is a defence for the defendant at whose suit that fault is actionable.[246]

For example, where a ship had out of date charts, that made it unseaworthy, and ship owners were in breach of their obligations under Art III r 1 of the Hague-Visby Rules (discussed more fully below). That was an actionable breach which led to the ship grounding when leaving port. In those circumstances, ship owners could not claim general average contributions from cargo interests.[247]

---

[245] York-Antwerp Rules, r D.

[246] *Strang, Steel & Co v Scott & Co* (1889) 14 App Cas 601 (PC); *Goulandris Bros Ltd v B Goldman & Sons Ltd* [1958] 1 QB 74 (QBD). Nevertheless, a contribution is still recoverable where the fault is exonerated by an exceptions clause: *The Carron Park* (1890) 15 PD 203; *Milburn & Co v Jamaica Fruit Importing and Trading Co of London* [1900] 2 QB 540 (CA).

[247] *The CMA CGM Libra* [2019] EWHC 481 (Adm); [2020] EWCA Civ 293.

Extraordinary sacrifice

The sacrifice or expenditure must be extraordinary. In *Robinson v Price*,[248] the ship sprang a leak, and needed continuous pumping, which used up its coal stores, so cargo had to be burned. This was an extraordinary sacrifice. In contrast, it is not extraordinary in time of war to require (the cost of) an escort tug to reduce the risk of attack.[249]

Other examples of extraordinary sacrifices might include jettisoning cargo,[250] for example to lighten a ship in danger of stranding, or damage done by water in putting out a fire,[251] or where the ship is deliberately stranded on shore.[252] In theory, salvage can be recoverable as general average,[253] but if the parties have separate liability to salvors, as is usually the case in practice, then salvage is only recoverable as general average on one of the listed rare occasions.[254] 'Special compensation' under art 14 of the Salvage Convention, or SCOPIC remuneration, in respect of environmental damage, is not allowed in general average.[255]

---

[248] (1877) 2 QBD 295 (CA).

[249] *Société Nouvelle d'Armement v Spillers & Bakers Ltd* [1917] 1 KB 865 (KBD).

[250] As long as it was carried in accordance with a recognised custom of the trade: York-Antwerp Rules, r I.

[251] York-Antwerp Rules, r III.

[252] York-Antwerp Rules, r V.

[253] York-Antwerp Rules, r VI(a). Note that there could be differences in assessment between salvage, where values are assessed at the place of safety, and general average, where values are usually assessed at the end of the common maritime adventure: York-Antwerp Rules, r G.1.

[254] York-Antwerp Rules, r VI(b).

Similarly, there is no allowance in general average for loss or expenses incurred in respect of damage to the environment,[256] or for demurrage or loss caused by reason of delay.[257]

General average need not involve physical damage to cargo. For example, where a ship carrying livestock needed to put into port for repairs in a country which meant that the livestock could no longer be sold in the UK as intended, and had to be sold more cheaply elsewhere, that loss was general average.[258] So too was a ransom paid to pirates.[259]

Substituted expenses

Following the adage 'a stitch in time saves nine', it may be possible to claim as 'substituted expenses' an expense which, by itself, would not amount to general average, but which thereby prevents a later general average event at least as costly.[260] An example might be temporary ship repairs.[261] Another is where ship owners incurred 51 days of extra running costs while they managed to negotiate a pirate's ransom down from US$6m to US$1.85.[262]

---

[255] York-Antwerp Rules, r VI(d).

[256] York-Antwerp Rules, r C.2.

[257] York-Antwerp Rules, r C.3.

[258] *Anglo-Argentine Live Stock and Produce Agency v Temperley Shipping Co* [1899] 2 QB 403 (QBD).

[259] *The Polar* [2020] EWHC 3318 (Comm).

[260] York-Antwerp Rules, r F.

[261] York-Antwerp Rules, r XIV.

[262] *The Longchamp* [2017] UKSC 68.

Intentional and reasonable

The general average act must be intentional. Damage caused by an accidental fire or its smoke is not allowable as general average, whereas water damage caused by putting out the fire is allowable.[263] To be intentional, there must be an element of choice. So for example, there was no general average for delay caused by a master's duty-bound compliance with the orders of a convoy commander.[264]

The general average act must also be reasonable – even if it remains hazardous. In *The Seapol*,[265] a ship in a gale was at risk of being dragged ashore and breaking her back. The master engaged in a risky manoeuvre to get the ship out to sea. The manoeuvre was successful – but the master damaged the ship and a pier in the process. Nevertheless, his actions were reasonable, and the damage caused was allowed as general average.

Danger

There must be actual danger.[266] A mistaken belief in danger that turns out to be non-existent will preclude a claim for general average.[267] In *The Makis*,[268] the ship

---

[263] York-Antwerp Rules, r III.

[264] *Athel Line Ltd v London & Liverpool War Risks Ins Assoc Ltd* [1944] KB 87 (KBD).

[265] [1934] P 53.

[266] A tidy analogy might be drawn with the need for danger in salvage.

[267] *Joseph Watson & Son Ltd v Fireman's Fund Ins Co* [1922] 2 KB 355 (KBD).

[268] *Vlassopoulos v British and Foreign Marine Ins Co* [1929] 1 KB 187 (KBD).

was at port when its foremast broke and fell on the main deck doing damage. Repairs were undertaken. These were not allowable as general average because the ship was never in danger. But during the subsequent voyage, the ship struck underwater wreckage and damaged its propeller, making it unfit to meet the ordinary perils of the sea. It put in for repairs at an interim port, and that cost was allowable as general average.

The general average act must be taken for the common safety. Thus, no interest need contribute where their safety was unaffected. For example, in *The Tagus*,[269] a ship ran aground on a coral reef, and lay in a dangerous position. Cargo A was trans-shipped. The ship then jettisoned further cargo, and incurred expenses in re-floating. Cargo A did not have to contribute to those subsequent expenses, because by then it was already safe.

If the common maritime adventure is ultimately unsuccessful, for example because the ship and its cargo are totally lost at sea by fire, then anything previously done is in effect redundant, and cannot be claimed as general average.[270]

---

[269] *Royal Mail Steam Packet Co Ltd v English Bank of Rio de Janeiro Ltd* (1887) 19 QBD 362 (DC).

[270] *Chellew v Royal Commission on the Sugar Supply* [1922] 1 KB 12 (CA). The technical reasoning in that case was as follows. The York-Antwerp Rules provide that contribution is based on the value of property at the termination of the adventure. If all property is lost, then its value is zero.

Possessory lien

The ship has a common law possessory lien over cargo for general average contributions, until paid or properly secured, and this lien must be exercised, not just to benefit the ship, but also by the ship to protect the other interests in the common maritime adventure.[271] Proper security tends to mean an average bond issued by cargo interests, along with an average guarantee provided by their insurers.[272] The ship itself does not have to provide security, but it might risk arrest. Cargo owners can also sue each other directly.[273] Indeed, average bonds and guarantees tend to be addressed to the ship and other interested parties to the adventure.

Just as the ship must exercise the lien, so too the ship owners must procure the average adjustment to be carried out.[274] An adjustment is usually done by a professional average adjuster. It is not binding, in contrast to a legal judgment, unless the parties otherwise agree. Rather, it can be challenged, and a second one procured.[275] That said, if the York-Antwerp Rules govern, and have been applied correctly, that much at least must be accepted.

---

[271] *Crooks & Co v Allan* (1879) 5 QBD 38 (QBD); *Strang, Steel & Co v Scott & Co* (1889) 14 App Cas 601 (PC); *Castle Insurance Co Ltd v Hong Kong Islands Shipping Co Ltd* [1984] AC 226 (PC), 234.

[272] *Castle Insurance Co Ltd v Hong Kong Islands Shipping Co Ltd* [1984] AC 226 (PC), 234. If a cash deposit is taken instead of a guarantee, it is held on terms governed by the York-Antwerp Rules, r XXII. The guarantee confers no greater rights than, as is coextensive with, the average bond: *The BSLE Sunrise* [2019] EWHC 2860 (Comm).

[273] *Strang, Steel & Co v Scott & Co* (1889) 14 App Cas 601 (PC).

[274] *Crooks & Co v Allan* (1879) 5 QBD 38 (QBD).

Law and jurisdiction

Since general average is usually provided for by contract, that same contract usually provides for a place of adjustment, which tends to import the law and practice of that place.[276] More often, the contract also has an express choice of law and jurisdiction or arbitration clause. The latter is apt to include general average disputes.[277] Average bonds and guarantees also tend to have an express choice of law and jurisdiction clause. The standard forms recommended by the CMI provide for English law and jurisdiction.[278]

There is a one-year time bar for bringing a claim for general average contribution, running from when the general average adjustment is issued, with a long-stop of 6 years from the end of the common maritime adventure.[279]

---

[275] *Wavertree Sailing Ship Co Ltd v Love* [1897] AC 373 (PC), 380; *Chandris v Argo Ins Co Ltd* [1963] 2 Lloyd's Rep 65 (Com Ct), 76; *Castle Insurance Co Ltd v Hong Kong Islands Shipping Co Ltd* [1984] AC 226 (PC), 238; *The Bijela* [1994] 2 All ER 289 (HL), 292.

[276] *Wavertree Sailing Ship Co Ltd v Love* [1897] AC 373 (PC), 381; *Union of India v EB Aaby's Rederi A/S* [1975] AC 797 (HL), 808-809.

[277] *The Astraea* [1971] 2 Lloyd's Rep 494 (Com Ct); *Union of India v EB Aaby's Rederi A/S* [1975] AC 797 (HL), 807.

[278] See the CMI's *Guidelines on General Average*. The CMI is the Comité Maritime International, an international organisation which brings together parties across the shipping industry, with a view to encouraging a unified approach to maritime law. It was responsible for drafting the York-Antwerp Rules 2016 (and the Limitation Convention).

[279] York-Antwerp Rules, r XXIII.

Chapter 8 – Time Charters

Employing a ship for a period of time

A time charter is a contract between a ship owner and a charterer whereby, for a period of time, the ship and its crew are put at the service of the charterer. The ship owner retains possession of the ship through their crew. (If the charterer provided their own crew instead, that would be a demise or bareboat charter, and the charterer would take possession.)[280] There are various standard form time charters. One of the most common is the New York Produce Exchange ('NYPE') form. NYPE 2015 contains 57 standard clauses, and we will consider the principal ones here.

Delivery. The ship will be hired from the time of delivery for a specified period of time.[281] The charter specifies a place for delivery.[282] Owners are to give advance notice of precisely when the ship will be delivered at the place specified. They must then give notice of delivery when the ship is in a position to come on hire.[283]

The time window for delivery is known as 'laydays'. Hire shall not commence before a specified time and date. Should the ship not have been

---

[280] NYPE 2015, cl 26, expressly provides that 'Nothing herein stated is to be construed as a demise of the Vessel to the Charterers'.

[281] NYPE 2015, cl 1(a).

[282] NYPE 2015, cl 2(a).

[283] NYPE 2015, cl 2(d). A notice of readiness invalidly given is of no effect, and does not become valid once the ship is actually ready (it must be re-given): *The Mexico 1* [1990] 1 Lloyd's Rep 507 (CA).

delivered before a specified end date and time, then charterers have the option of cancelling the charter party any time up to notice of delivery.[284] If the cancelling date passes without that option being exercised, owners still remain obliged to tender delivery of the ship with reasonable despatch.[285]

Redelivery. 'The Vessel shall be redelivered to the Owners in like good order and condition, ordinary wear and tear excepted...' at a specified place.[286] Early redelivery is a repudiatory breach. Owners can choose to keep the contract alive, and continue to charge hire, unless the decision to do so is wholly unreasonable.[287]

What about late redelivery? First, charterers are to give advance notice of redelivery, after which they shall give 'only such further employment orders, if any, as are reasonably expected when given to allow redelivery to occur on or before the date notified'.[288] Otherwise their orders are illegitimate, and owners can refuse them, instead calling for alternative orders, which if not forthcoming could be a repudiatory breach.[289]

---

[284] NYPE 2015, cl 3. Cancellation does not depend on breach: *The Madeleine* [1967] 2 Lloyd's Rep 224 (Com Ct), 239.

[285] *Moel Tryvan Ship Co Ltd v Andrew Weir & Co* [1910] 2 KB 844 (CA); *The Democritos* [1976] 2 Lloyd's Rep 149 (CA).

[286] NYPE 2015, cl 4(a).

[287] *Aquafaith* [2012] 2 Lloyd's Rep 61 (Com Ct).

[288] NYPE 2015, cl 4(b). Charterers' obligations to give legitimate orders at the end of the time charter are mirrored at the beginning of the time charter by owners' obligations to allow to be given only such employment orders as are reasonably compatible with the notified date of delivery: cl 2(d).

[289] *The Gregos* [1995] 1 Lloyd's Rep 1 (HL).

Second, if the ship is on its last voyage when the time period ends, that does not automatically terminate the charter party. Rather, charterers are still obliged to pay hire.[290] Indeed, if last voyage orders are legitimate, but the voyage overruns, charterers have an express contractual entitlement to continue to use the ship, at the charter party hire rate or (if higher) the prevailing market rate.[291]

Payment of hire. 'Charterers shall pay for the use and hire of the said Vessel' at a daily rate, or pro rata for part of a day, from delivery until redelivery.[292] The first payment of hire is due on delivery, and hire is to be paid 15 days in advance (that is, to cover the following 15 days).[293] If payment is not made on time, charterers shall be given 3 banking days written notice to rectify the failure,[294] failing which owners shall be entitled to withdraw (permanently) the ship from service and seek damages.[295] Owners can also withhold (suspend) performance while hire is outstanding, during which time hire continues to accrue.[296] If hire is overpaid, for example because the ship goes off-hire during the following 15 days, owners must

---

[290] *The London Explorer* [1971] 1 Lloyd's Rep 523 (HL).

[291] NYPE 2015, cl 52(a) – but only where the minimum period of the charter exceeds 5 months. See too: *The Johnny* [1977] 2 Lloyd's Rep 1 (CA), where the relevant market rate is not a voyage charter comparable to this last voyage, but the current rate for a time charter of this overall length.

[292] NYPE 2015, cl 10.

[293] NYPE 2015, cl 11(a).

[294] NYPE 2015, cl 11(b).

[295] NYPE 2015, cl 11(c). Withdrawal means the termination of the charter party: *The Agios Giorgis* [1976] 2 Lloyd's Rep 192 (Com Ct).

[296] NYPE 2015, cl 11(d).

repay any hire which was unearned,[297] and charterers might make an adjustment to the following hire payment.[298]

Off-hire. The payment of hire shall cease for the time lost due to various off-hire events.[299] Bunkers used by the ship while off-hire are for owners' account. Such off-hire events include: deficiency or default or strike of crew;[300] deficiency of stores; fire; breakdown of, or damage to hull, machinery or equipment;[301] grounding; arrest of the ship (unless caused by events for which charterers are responsible); detention by average accidents[302] to the ship or cargo (unless resulting from inherent vice, defect or quality of the cargo); drydocking;[303] or any

---

[297] *The Trident Beauty* [1994] 1 Lloyd's Rep 365 (HL). Note that NYPE 2015, cl 23, also expressly provides that any overpaid hire is 'to be returned at once'.

[298] *The Nanfri* [1978] 2 Lloyd's Rep 132 (CA), appealed on a different point at [1979] AC 757 (HL). Note too that NYPE 2015, cl 17, provides that time lost due to reduced speed 'may be deducted from the hire'. There might also be a right to an equitable set-off where owners have wrongfully withheld service: *Geldof Metaalconstructie NV v Simon Carves Ltd* [2011] 1 Lloyd's Rep 517 (CA).

[299] NYPE 2015, cl 17.

[300] As for industrial action, see too NYPE 2015, cl 41. 'Default' does not include negligence: *The Saldanha* [2011] 1 Lloyd's Rep 187 (Com Ct).

[301] Disabled cargo handling gear is explicitly an off-hire event as well under NYPE 2015, cl 28.

[302] 'Average accident' merely means an accident which causes damage: *The Mareva AS* [1977] 1 Lloyd's Rep 368 (Com Ct), 381; *The Saldanha* [2011] 1 Lloyd's Rep 187 (Com Ct), [11]. It does not refer to general average.

[303] By NYPE 2015, cl 19, except in case of emergency, no drydocking shall take place during the currency of the charter party. But by cl 52(b), drydocking is permitted where the minimum period of the time charter exceeds 5 months.

other similar cause preventing the full working of the ship.[304] This final phrase has the effect of qualifying all the prior-listed off-hire events, requiring them too to prevent the full working of the ship.[305] What matters is that the ship is unable to perform fully the next service required of it.[306] Any defect which does not affect what the ship is currently doing need not amount to off-hire.[307]

Hire is also suspended if the ship deviates or puts back, contrary to charterers' orders, for any reason other than accident to cargo, or salvage,[308] until the ship is again in an equidistant position and the voyage resumed. Charterers have the option of adding any off-hire time to the charter period, if such option is properly declared.[309]

---

[304] If requisitioned, the vessel is off-hire, and after 90 days either party has the option of cancelling the charter: NYPE 2015, cl 36. If the ship is seized by pirates, hire payments also cease after 90 days: cl 39(f). There are further clauses dealing explicitly with stowaways, cl 42, and smuggling, cl 43.

[305] *The Mareva AS* [1977] 1 Lloyd's Rep 368 (Com Ct), 382. 'Preventing the full working' means that the ship is prevented from working at 100%. Anything less than 100% can result in off-hire. It is not necessary that the ship is unable to work at all.

[306] *The Berge Sund* [1993] 2 Lloyd's Rep 453 (CA), 460. In that case it was said that, because the ship was not clean enough to receive cargo, the next service required of it was cleaning, and the ship was able to do that.

[307] *Hogarth v Miller, Bro & Co* [1891] AC 48 (HL). In that case, although the ship was undergoing repairs to its engines, this did not prevent it from being fully efficient in the task at hand of discharging cargo.

[308] NYPE 2015, cl 22, gives the ship liberty to assist vessels in distress, and to deviate for the purpose of saving life and property. A similar liberty is provided by the Hague Rules, Art IV r 4, incorporated through the General Clause Paramount (discussed below). By cl 24, all salvage shall be for the equal benefit of owners and charterers, after deducting expenses and the crew's proportion.

[309] NYPE 2015, cl 52(c).

Condition on delivery. 'The Vessel on delivery shall be seaworthy and in every way fit to be employed for the intended service...', with a full complement of qualified crew.[310] While this seems like an absolute or strict obligation, the incorporation of the General Clause Paramount (discussed below), has the effect of softening the obligation, so that owners must exercise *due diligence* to deliver the ship in a seaworthy condition.[311] Seaworthy also means cargoworthy,[312] and legally fit in terms of having the necessary documentation.[313]

Maintenance. Owners 'shall maintain the Vessel's class and keep her in a thoroughly efficient state...for and during the service', and with a full complement of crew.[314] Again, although this looks like an absolute or strict obligation, in fact owners are obliged only to take reasonable steps to maintain the ship.[315] This will

---

[310] NYPE 2015, cl 2(b).

[311] *The Fjord Wind* [2000] 2 Lloyd's Rep 191 (CA).

[312] See too NYPE 2015, cl 2(c), which provides that the ship's holds shall be clean and in all respects ready to receive the intended cargo. There is a mirror requirement that charterers redeliver the ship with clean holds, with an option of paying a lump sum instead of cleaning: cl 10.

[313] *Ciampa v British India Steam Navigation Co Ltd* [1915] 2 KB 774 (KBD) (unseaworthy because no deratisation certificate); *The Madeleine* [1967] 2 Lloyd's Rep 224 (Com Ct) (not seaworthy as deratisation certificate expired); *The Derby* [1985] 2 Lloyd's Rep 325 (CA) (no need for an ITF blue card).

[314] NYPE 2015, cl 6(a). Also, owners are to maintain the cargo handling gear: cl 28.

[315] *Tynedale Steam Shipping Co Ltd v Anglo-Soviet Shipping Co Ltd* (1936) 54 Ll L Rep 341 (CA), 344-345; *Snia v Suzuki & Co* (1923) 17 Ll L Rep 78 (KBD), 88. This is consistent with the requirement in the Hague Rules, incorporated through the General Clause Paramount (discussed below), to use due diligence to make the ship seaworthy for each voyage.

require the ship to be inspected regularly, which will often reveal a need for repair.[316] It is not enough that owners appoint a competent contractor to carry out the repair work; rather, the repair work itself must also be carried out with due diligence.[317]

While the ship is on-hire, charterers are to pay for such things as bunkers (fuel),[318] port charges,[319] pilots, and canal dues.[320] Owners are to provide and pay for such things as the insurance of the ship, all provisions, and crew wages, and provide all necessary documentation.[321]

Speed and fuel consumption. 'Upon delivery and throughout the duration of this Charter Party the Vessel shall be capable of [specified] speed and daily consumption rates...in good weather on all sea passages...'.[322] It is a defence if any under-performance is due to compliance with charterers' orders, for example, trading in a tropical zone so that the hull becomes fouled with barnacles.[323]

---

[316] *Smith, Hogg & Co Ltd v Black Sea & Baltic General Ins Co Ltd* (1939) 64 Ll L Rep 87 (CA), 89.

[317] *The Muncaster Castle* [1961] 1 Lloyd's Rep 57 (HL).

[318] Ordinarily, charterers take over and pay for bunkers on delivery, and owners take over bunkers on redelivery: see NYPE 2015, cl 9, which also specifies the quality of bunkers.

[319] And local taxes: NYPE 2015, cl 40.

[320] NYPE 2015, cl 7.

[321] NYPE 2015, cl 6. Additional clauses deal with specific documentary requirements, like international safety management, cl 44, international ship and port facility security code, cl 45, and advance cargo notification, cl 48-50.

[322] NYPE 2015, cl 12(a). Good weather is expressly defined as wind up to Force 4 on the Beaufort Scale, and up to Sea State 3 on the Douglas Sea Scale.

[323] *The Pamphilos* [2002] 2 Lloyd's Rep 681 (Com Ct), 690-691.

Also, 'the Master shall perform the voyages with due despatch...'.[324] If the master deliberately chooses a slower route, for example because of a preference for calmer weather rather than safety, that might be a breach of charter.[325] However, if the voyage takes longer on account of an error in navigation, then owners might be able to rely on the exceptions clauses (see below).[326]

If the speed is reduced, or fuel consumption increased, then charterers can submit a documented claim, which if not agreed shall be sent to an independent expert.[327] Additionally, 'If upon the voyage the speed be reduced by defect in, or breakdown of, any part of her hull, machinery or equipment, the time so lost, and the cost of any extra bunkers consumed...may be deducted from hire'.[328]

Safe ports. During the period of the charter party, 'the Vessel shall be employed in such lawful trades between safe ports and safe places within the following trading limits...as the Charterers shall direct'.[329] It is a breach by charterers to

---

[324] NYPE 2015, cl 8(a). Charterers can ask the ship to reduce speed to meet a specified time of arrival: cl 38.

[325] *The Hill Harmony* [2001] 1 Lloyd's Rep 147 (HL).

[326] In *The Pearl C* [2012] 2 Lloyd's Rep 533 (Com Ct), a distinction was noted between a deliberate decision to proceed slowly, which was not covered by the exceptions, and negligence in navigation or management, which was caught by the exceptions introduced by the General Paramount Clause.

[327] NYPE 2015, cl 12. Where the ship has an extended stay in a tropical zone in accordance with charterers' orders, with attendant risks of hull fouling, then speed and consumption warranties are suspended pending inspection and cleaning: cl 30. Owners shall also exercise due diligence to ensure that the ship is operated in a manner which minimises fuel consumption: cl 38.

[328] NYPE 2015, cl 17.

[329] NYPE 2015, cl 1(b). See further NYPE 2015, cl 1(c), which provides that the Vessel shall be loaded

order the ship outside those limits, but if the ship obeys, owners may be entitled to hire at the market rate for such trades, rather than the charter party rate.[330]

A port will not be safe unless this ship can reach it, use it and return from it without, in the absence of some abnormal occurrence, being exposed to danger which cannot be avoided by good navigation and seamanship.[331] It is not simply about physical safety; a port can also be politically unsafe, for example because it is the site of a rebellion making the ship liable to confiscation.[332] A port is not unsafe where, for example, two regular characteristics, such as long waves and gale force winds, unexpectedly combine for a rare casualty.[333]

The port must be prospectively safe, meaning that, at the time when the order to proceed there is given, it will be safe for the ship upon arrival. If the port becomes unsafe while the ship is there, due to an abnormal occurrence, then charterers incur no liability (it is a matter for owners' insurers). But if the port

---

and discharged in any safe place that the Charterers may direct. There is an additional war risks clause, cl 34, and piracy clause, cl 39, which entitles the ship to refuse to enter a danger zone, and to leave any place which has become dangerous. See too cl 46, where the ship need not comply with orders which expose the ship to any sanction. Also, the vessel shall not be obliged to force ice, or enter an icebound port: cl 35. 'Lawful trades' probably refers to what is lawful by the country of the ship's flag and the countries which the ship visits.

[330] *Rederi Sverre Hansen AS v PHS Van Ommeren* (1921) 6 Ll L Rep 193 (CA); *The Batis* [1990] 1 Lloyd's Rep 345 (Com Ct).

[331] *The Eastern City* [1958] 2 Lloyd's Rep 127 (CA).

[332] *Ogden v Graham* (1861) 1 B & S 773, 121 ER 901.

[333] *The Ocean Victory* [2017] UKSC 35, [2017] 1 WLR 1793.

becomes unsafe prior to arrival, owners can refuse to proceed there, and charterers must issue new orders.[334]

Charterers' orders. Beyond the question of safe ports, more broadly 'The Master...shall be under the order and directions of the Charterers as regards employment and agency'.[335] This normally implies a term that charterers will indemnify owners for the consequences of following their orders, unless there is an intervening act, or it is a risk which owners have contractually accepted,[336] such as:

'Owners shall remain responsible for the navigation of the Vessel...'.[337] In terms of where a ship might proceed, it can be a fine line between questions of employment and questions of navigation. For example, while a master might legitimately prefer a different route from the one requested by charterers, for reasons of navigational safety, nevertheless the master cannot simply prefer calmer weather when the ship is expected to endure adverse weather as part of its employment.[338]

---

[334] *The Evia (No 2)* [1982] 2 Lloyd's Rep 307 (HL).

[335] NYPE 2015, cl 8(a). See too NYPE 2015, cl 15, which states that charterers shall furnish the master with all requisite instructions and sailing directions. And NYPE 2015, cl 12(b), whereby the master shall comply with the reporting procedure of the charterers' weather routing service and shall follow routing recommendations, provided that the safety of the vessel or cargo is not compromised.

[336] *The Island Archon* [1994] 2 Lloyd's Rep 227 (CA).

[337] NYPE 2015, cl 26, which also provides that, although charterers are to pay for pilots and tugs (by cl 7(a)), owners remain responsible for the navigation decisions of pilots and tugs.

[338] *The Hill Harmony* [2001] 1 Lloyd's Rep 147 (HL).

Cargo. As for loading and discharging, 'Charterers shall perform all cargo handling...at their risk and expense, under the supervision of the Master'.[339] The latter phrase allows the master to intervene to protect the safety of the ship and cargo.[340] As for the type of cargo to be carried, 'The Vessel shall be employed in carrying lawful merchandise' excluding dangerous goods unless carried in accordance with formal requirements.[341]

'Cargo claims as between the Owners and the Charterers shall be settled in accordance with the Inter-Club NYPE Agreement...'.[342] That scheme provides a rough and ready means for allocating responsibility. In broad terms, cargo claims arising out of unseaworthiness or fault in navigation or management of the ship are borne 100% by owners, cargo claims arising out of the handling of the cargo are borne 100% by charterers, and other claims are borne 50% each.

---

[339] NYPE 2015, cl 8(a). Additionally, charterers shall pay for all damage to the ship caused by stevedores: cl 37. The whole reach of the ship's holds and decks shall be at charterers' disposal, cl 13(a), but owners are to be indemnified by charterers for carrying any deck cargo, cl 13(b). Bills of lading shall also be claused to the effect that deck cargo is at the risk, not of the ship owners, but of charterers and cargo interests, cl 31(c).

[340] It is common enough to see the standard form amended to read 'under the supervision *and responsibility* of the master', which usually transfers risk back to owners: *The Shinjitsu Maru No 5* [1985] 1 Lloyd's Rep 568 (Com Ct).

[341] NYPE 2015, cl 16. See also cl 29, which requires charterers to provide appropriate information such that dangerous cargoes can be carried safely, failing which the master can refuse the cargo. On dangerous goods, see too the Hague-Visby Rules, Art IV r 6, which apply by virtue of the General Clause Paramount, cl 33(a).

[342] NYPE 2015, cl 27.

Bills of lading. 'The Master shall sign bills of lading…for cargo as presented in conformity with mates' receipts'.[343] Charterers may sign on behalf of the master with the latter's prior written authority. Electronic bills of lading may be issued too.[344]

Charterers can produce bills of lading which incur greater liability for the owners as carriers than the charter party itself provides, but this is accompanied by at least an implied indemnity against the consequences.[345] The NYPE form makes this indemnity express.[346] The master can in some cases refuse to sign bills of lading, for example, which would require the ship to trade outside the contractual trading limits.[347] Bills of lading are to contain various protective clauses including the General Clause Paramount.[348]

Exceptions. The following are 'always mutually excepted':[349] act of God; enemies;[350] fire; restraint of princes, rulers and people; and all dangers and

---

[343] NYPE 2015, cl 31(a).

[344] NYPE 2015, cl 32.

[345] *The Island Archon* [1994] 2 Lloyd's Rep 227 (CA).

[346] NYPE 2015, cl 31(b).

[347] *Halcyon Steamship Co Ltd v Continental Grain Co* (1943) 75 Ll L Rep 80 (CA), 84. Other examples might include: where the quantity or quality of the cargo is clearly mis-described, or when the bills wrongly record that the cargo is carried under deck (rather than on deck).

[348] NYPE 2015, cl 33.

[349] NYPE 2015, cl 21.

[350] There is an additional war risks clause, cl 34, and piracy clause, cl 39, which entitles the ship to refuse to enter a danger zone, and to leave any place which has become dangerous. See too cl 46, where the ship need not comply with orders which expose the ship to any sanction.

accidents of the seas, rivers, machinery, boilers and navigation; and errors of navigation.

Nothing in the foregoing list excepts liability for negligence.[351] However, the General Clause Paramount (see below) does add further exceptions including: *neglect* of the master in the navigation or management of the ship; seizure under legal process; insufficiency of packing; latent defects not discoverable by due diligence; and any other cause arising without the actual fault and privity of the carrier and without the fault or neglect of the agents or servants of the carrier. These exceptions from the General Clause Paramount are not available if caused by owners' failure to exercise due diligence to make the ship seaworthy.[352]

Lien. 'The Owners shall have a lien upon all cargoes, sub-hires and sub-freights...belonging or due to the Charterers or any sub-charterers...for any amounts due under this Charter Party, including general average contributions, and the Charterers shall have a lien on the Vessel for all monies paid in advance and not earned...'.[353] If owners exercise their lien, hire continues to be payable.[354] (Owners may also be able to collect freight under the bill of lading contract.)[355]

---

[351] This is because those exceptions could apply to circumstances other than negligence. For this general principle, see: *Canada Steamship Lines Ltd v The King* [1952] AC 192 (PC).

[352] *Maxine Footwear Co Ltd v Canadian Government Merchant Marine Ltd* [1959] 2 Lloyd's Rep 105 (PC).

[353] NYPE 2015, cl 23. Charterers also promise not to procure any necessaries on the credit of owners, by cl 23, so as to avoid creating any maritime lien over the ship.

[354] *The Chrysovalandou Dyo* [1981] 1 Lloyd's Rep 159 (Com Ct).

[355] But in this regard, see too: *The Bulk Chile* [2013] 2 Lloyd's Rep 38 (CA), [28] (owners perhaps

General average clause.[356] General average shall be adjusted according to the York-Antwerp Rules and settled in the same place as stipulated in the law and arbitration clause.[357] Charterers shall also procure that all bills of lading issued during the currency of the charter contain a clause requiring cargo interests to contribute in general average, adjusted according to the York-Antwerp Rules.[358]

General Clause Paramount. The General Clause Paramount 'shall be deemed to form part of this Charter Party', and it is to be contained in all issued bills of lading.[359] The General Clause Paramount itself says that the US Carriage of Good by Sea Act or Hague Rules or Hague-Visby Rules,[360] as applicable, as may mandatorily apply, are incorporated. If none are mandatorily applicable, then the Hague Rules shall apply.

---

cannot collect freight where hire continues to be paid); *The Nanfri* [1978] 2 Lloyd's Rep 132 (CA) (charterers entitled to issue freight pre-paid bills).

[356] NYPE 2015, cl 25.

[357] The standard options for law and arbitration under NYPE 2015, cl 54, are arbitration in New York under US maritime law, or in London under English law, or in Singapore under either English or Singaporean law.

[358] Such a clause is called a 'New Jason Clause' – see NYPE 2015, cl 33(c). It also requires cargo interests to pay salvage.

[359] NYPE 2015, cl 33(a).

[360] Those three regimes are largely similar, except that: the limits of liability are different in each; and the time limit wording is different in the Hague-Visby Rules, although all three regimes have a principal time limit of one year.

The effect of the General Clause Paramount is to apply the Hague Rules regime, not just to bills of lading issued under the charter party, but to the charter party itself, and to all its voyages, and to all its activities.[361]

There is a fuller discussion of the Hague Rules regime in the chapter on bills of lading. For present purposes, the main effect of the regime on the charter party is as follows. It reduces owners' otherwise seemingly strict liability to deliver the ship in a seaworthy condition, to an obligation to use due diligence to make the ship seaworthy.[362] It extends the exceptions to include the negligence of the master in the navigation or management of the ship.[363] It introduces a one-year time limit for claims in respect of goods,[364] and provides a limit of liability for cargo claims.[365] However, the latter provisions are trumped by the NYPE Inter-Club Agreement.[366]

---

[361] Despite the language of Art II of the Hague Rules being couched in terms of the carriage of goods: *Anglo-Saxon Petroleum Co Ltd v Adamastos Shipping Co Ltd* [1958] 1 Lloyd's Rep 73 (HL); *The Satya Kailash* [1984] 1 Lloyd's Rep 588 (CA).

[362] *The Fjord Wind* [2000] 2 Lloyd's Rep 191 (CA).

[363] Hague Rules, Art IV r 2(a).

[364] Hague Rules, Art III r 6; *The Marinor* [1996] 1 Lloyd's Rep 301 (Com Ct).

[365] Hague Rules, Art IV r 5.

[366] *The Strathnewton* [1983] 1 Lloyd's Rep 219 (CA); *The Benlawers* [1989] 2 Lloyd's Rep 51 (Com Ct).

Chapter 9 – Voyage Charters

Carrying cargo by ship

A voyage charter is a contract between a ship owner who agrees to carry cargo from one place to another, and a charterer who agrees to procure the cargo and pay the owner a fee ('freight'). As with time charters, so too with voyage charters, there are various standard form contracts. Perhaps the most common is the Uniform General Charter ('GENCON'). GENCON 1994 contains two parts. Part I consists of boxes to be filled in with the details of this particular voyage. Part II are the general terms. There are 19 general clauses, and we will consider some of the principal ones in this chapter.

Clause 1. The ship is 'now in position as stated…and expected ready to load…about the date indicated'. 'About' gives a margin of error, perhaps of a few days.[367] The date when the ship is expected ready to load must be given honestly and on reasonable grounds.[368]

The ship shall 'as soon as her prior commitments have been completed, proceed to the loading port…or so near thereto as she may safely get'. Ordinarily there would be an implied term that the ship would proceed to the loading port with despatch, so as to arrive with reasonable certainty by the expected date.[369]

---

[367] *Monroe Bros Ltd v Ryan* [1935] 2 KB 28 (CA), 37 (+ 3 days); *Louis Dreyfus & Co v Lauro* (1938) 60 Ll L Rep 94 (KBD) (+ 4 days).

[368] *Samuel Sanday & Co v Keighley, Maxted & Co* (1922) 27 Com Cas 296 (CA); *The Mihalis Angelos* [1971] 1 QB 164 (CA).

However, GENCON 1994 makes that dependent on the ship having completed its prior commitments. As for that, there may be an implied term such that no prior commitments are to be entered into by the ship owner which preclude the estimated date of readiness from being reasonably achievable.[370]

Should the ship not be ready to load on the specified cancelling date, charterers have the option of cancelling the charter party.[371] This right of cancellation is not dependent on the fault of owners. But if charterers want to sue for compensation, then they will need to show a breach of charter by owners, such as the expected readiness date was not given honestly or reasonably, or the ship did not proceed to the loading port with reasonable despatch.

At the loading port, the ship shall 'there load a full and complete cargo…which the Charterers bind themselves to ship'. Charterers are under a strict obligation to procure cargo.[372] If charterers procure less than a full cargo, ship owners can claim for the shortfall ('deadfreight'). The charter party might expressly stipulate a maximum and minimum quantity of cargo, for example 'not less than 500 tonnes, not more than 1000 tonnes'. This does not provide an option

---

[369] *Monroe Bros Ltd v Ryan* [1935] 2 KB 28 (CA); *Louis Dreyfus & Co v Lauro* (1938) 60 Ll L Rep 94 (KBD); *The Pacific Voyager* [2018] EWCA Civ 2413.

[370] *Evera SA Comercial v North Shipping Co Ltd* [1956] 2 Lloyd's Rep 367 (QBD); *The Pacific Voyager* [2018] EWCA Civ 2413.

[371] GENCON 1994, cl 9(a). By clause 9(b), owners have a one-off chance to ask for a substitute later cancelling date where they anticipate that the ship will not be ready to load in time. Owners can cancel for war risks, cl 17, and the charter might be null and void if the loading port is inaccessible due to ice, cl 18.

[372] See too *The Aello* [1961] AC 135 (HL).

of how much to load: a full cargo must be loaded, but ship owners are warranting that a full load will not be less than 500 tonnes, and not more than 1000 tonnes.[373]

There is an implied term not to ship dangerous cargo unless ship owners have given informed consent.[374] If the cargo is expressly named in the charter party, but this particular cargo, although it appears to match the description, nevertheless has characteristics making it unusually dangerous, again notice of those dangers must be given.[375]

Once the ship is loaded, it shall 'proceed to the discharging port…as ordered on signing Bills of Lading, or so near thereto as she may safely get'. The phrase 'as ordered' means that charterers must give orders identifying the discharge port (if not already identified) no later than upon the signing of the bills of lading.[376]

There is an implied obligation on ship owners to proceed to the discharge port with reasonable despatch and by the usual route without deviation.[377] While GENCON 1994 does expressly grant a 'liberty to call at any port in any order',[378] this should still be ports substantially *en route*.[379]

---

[373] *Jardine Matheson & Co v Clyde Shipping Co* [1910] 1 KB 627 (KBD); *Noemijulia Steamship Co Ltd v Minister of Food* [1951] 1 KB 223, 226.

[374] *Brass v Maitland* (1856) 6 El & Bl 470, 119 ER 940; *Bamfield v Goole & Sheffield Transport Co Ltd* [1910] 2 KB 94; *Giannis NK* [1998] 1 Lloyd's Rep 337 (HL).

[375] *The Athanasia Comninos* [1990] 1 Lloyd's Rep 277 (Com Ct), 283.

[376] *A/S Tank v Agence Maritime L Strauss* (1939) 64 Ll L Rep 19 (KBD).

[377] *Reardon Smith Line Ltd v Black Sea and Baltic General Ins Co Ltd* [1939] AC 562 (HL); *The Kriti Rex* [1996] 2 Lloyd's Rep 171 (Com Ct); *The Hill Harmony* [2001] 1 Lloyd's Rep 147 (HL); *The Santa Isabella* [2019] EWHC 3152 (Comm).

Must the loading or discharging port be safe? The reference to 'so near thereto as the ship may safely get' does not imply any safe port warranty.[380] Instead, it might provide the ship with a liberty to proceed to a different nearby port if there is a supervening event (perhaps akin to frustration) which prevents the ship attaining the original port.[381]

Owners' responsibility.[382] 'The Owners are to be responsible for loss of or damage to the goods or for delay in delivery of the goods only...[where] caused by personal want of due diligence on the part of the Owners or their Manager to make the Vessel in all respects seaworthy...or by the personal act or default of the Owners or their Manager.'

Under the Hague Rules, the duty to exercise due diligence to make the ship seaworthy is non-delegable.[383] So if ship owners appoint another party to make the ship seaworthy, if that other party fails to exercise due diligence, then owners are themselves liable. In contrast, GENCON 1994 makes the duty delegable. So if owners exercise due diligence in their choice of appointing another party to make the ship seaworthy, then that is good enough, even if that

---

[378] GENCON 1994, cl 3, which also gives a liberty to assist other ships, and to deviate for the purpose of saving life or property.

[379] *Leduc & Co v Ward* (1888) 20 QBD 475 (CA); *Glynn v Margetson & Co* [1893] AC 351 (HL).

[380] *The APJ Priti* [1987] 2 Lloyd's Rep 37 (CA).

[381] *Dahl & Co v Nelson* (1880) 6 App Cas 38 (HL) (delay in waiting for space at the port); *The Athamas* [1963] 1 Lloyd's Rep 287 (CA) (pilots would not take ship any closer to port).

[382] GENCON 1994, cl 2.

[383] *The Muncaster Castle* [1961] AC 807 (HL).

other party fails to do their job properly.[384] That is the effect of the reference to 'personal' fault.[385]

Owners are probably only liable in respect of *foreseeable* harm caused by their personal fault.[386] But the protections of this clause do not extend to misdescriptions of the ship at the time of contracting.[387]

'Owners are not responsible for loss, damage or delay arising from any other cause whatsoever, even from the neglect or default of the Master or crew or some other person employed by the Owners on board or ashore...or from unseaworthiness...'. Following on from the first half of this clause, this second half still only applies to loss, damage or delay *to the goods* (despite the absence of repetition of those words).[388]

Freight. Freight is the fee payable for carrying the cargo. It is usually paid at a stated rate calculated on the in-taken quantity of cargo.[389] If freight is to be paid on shipment, it shall be deemed earned and non-returnable, ship or cargo lost or not lost.[390] Owners shall not be required to sign bills of lading showing freight prepaid unless the freight due has actually been paid.[391] If freight is payable at destination,

---

[384] *The Brabant* [1965] 2 Lloyd's Rep 546 (Com Ct).

[385] 'Personal fault' usually refers to the fault of a company director or perhaps senior manager, rather than lower-level employee.

[386] *The Eurus* [1998] 1 Lloyd's Rep 351 (CA).

[387] *The TFL Prosperity* [1984] 1 Lloyd's Rep 123 (HL).

[388] *The Dominator* [1959] 1 QB 498 (QBD), reversed on another point [1960] 2 QB 49 (CA).

[389] GENCON 1994, cl 4(a).

[390] GENCON 1994, cl 4(b).

it shall not be deemed earned until the cargo is delivered, and charterers shall have the option of paying freight on the delivered quantity.[392] Claims by charterers cannot be off-set against freight, which must be paid in full.[393] (Charterers can of course bring separate proceedings seeking compensation from owners for any breach of charter.)

Loading and discharging. The common law rule is that charterers are responsible to bring cargo alongside, and up to the ship's rail, and then the ship must take it from the rail and stow it.[394] GENCON 1994 makes the position far more clear cut. The cargo shall be loaded, stowed and discharged by charterers, free of any risk, liability or expense to owners.[395] Owners shall give free use of the ship's cargo handling gear, and time lost by breakdown of the gear shall not count as laytime or demurrage.[396] Charterers shall be responsible for damage to the ship caused by

---

[391] GENCON 1994, cl 4(b).

[392] GENCON 1994, cl 4(c).

[393] *The Aries* [1977] 1 Lloyd's Rep 334 (HL); *The Khian Captain (No. 2)* [1986] 1 Lloyd's Rep 429 (Com Ct). The rule that freight cannot be off-set does not apply to freight forwarders who procure the carriage of goods, but do not carry or pay for the carriage themselves: *Globalink Transportation and Logistics Worldwide LLP v DHL Project & Chartering Ltd* [2019] EWHC 225 (Comm).

[394] *Harris v Best, Ryley & Co* (1892) 68 LT 76 (CA).

[395] GENCON 1994, cl 5(a). Where the Hague Rules are incorporated into the charter party, for example through a paramount clause, then although Art III r 2 provides that *the carrier* shall properly and carefully load, stow and discharge the goods, the parties are free to allocate those tasks to charterers: *Pyrene Co Ltd v Scindia Navigation Co Ltd* [1954] 2 QB 402 (QBD), 417-418; *GH Renton & Co Ltd v Palmyra Trading Corp of Panama* [1957] AC 149 (HL).

[396] GENCON 1994, cl 5(b).

stevedores. Charterers are obliged to repair any stevedore damage, and any time so lost shall be paid to owners at the demurrage rate.[397]

Laytime. The cargo shall be loaded and discharged within the stated number of running days or hours, weather permitting, Sundays and holidays excepted, unless used in which case time is to count.[398] 'Running hours' means that, once started, time keeps running continuously, day and night.[399] If weather would prevent loading, then laytime stops running, even if the ship would have been prevented from loading for other reasons (for example, because the berth is occupied).[400] Loading includes stowing and all other cargo operations necessary to allow the ship to sail.[401] Once the ship is loaded, there is an implied obligation on charterers to complete formalities such that the ship can depart promptly, even if some laytime remains unused.[402]

Laytime commences at a set hour after notice of readiness is given by the ship, but any time used before then counts.[403] The ship must be actually ready.[404] The notice does not become valid retrospectively; it must be re-given.[405] (There

---

[397] GENCON 1994, cl 5(c).

[398] GENCON 1994, cl 6(a), (b). For the affect of strikes on laytime and demurrage, see cl 16.

[399] *Neilsen & Co v Wait, James & Co* (1885) 16 QBD 67 (CA), 72.

[400] *The Vorras* [1983] 1 Lloyd's Rep 579 (CA).

[401] *Argonaut Navigation Co Ltd v Ministry of Food* (1948) 82 Ll L Rep 223 (CA).

[402] *The Nolisement* [1917] 1 KB 160 (CA).

[403] GENCON 1994, cl 6(c).

[404] *The Linardos* [1994] 1 Lloyd's Rep 28 (Com Ct).

[405] *The Mexico 1* [1990] 1 Lloyd's Rep 507 (CA). So too, a notice of readiness given outside the

are further provisions if, upon the ship's arrival at the port, the berth is not available.)[406]

Demurrage. It is a breach of contract by charterers to take longer to load and discharge than is allowed by laytime. Demurrage is liquidated damages, that is, a specified rate of payment for that breach.[407] Demurrage falls due day by day and is payable upon receipt of owners' invoice. If not paid, owners shall give 96 running hours written notice to rectify the failure. If not so rectified, and the ship is at the loading port, owners are entitled to terminate the charter party and claim damages.[408] This provision otherwise precludes owners from terminating the charter party simply because laytime has been exceeded, until the delay amounts to frustration.[409] It does not matter why laytime has been exceeded, in other words, it does not matter what breach of charter has been committed by charterers, if the only consequence is delay in loading or discharging, it is the demurrage provision which applies (and not unliquidated damages for detention).[410]

---

prescribed office hours is a nullity: *The Alpha Harmony* [2019] EWHC 2522 (Comm).

[406] GENCON 1994, cl 6(c).

[407] *The Forum Craftsman* [1991] 1 Lloyd's Rep 81 (Com Ct), 87.

[408] GENCON 1994, cl 7, which says that owners can terminate 'at any time', although it may be that owners lose the right to terminate (for example, by waiver or estoppel) through delay or contrary behaviour.

[409] *Universal Cargo Carriers Corp v Citati* [1957] 2 QB 401 (QBD), affirmed on a different point [1957] 1 WLR 979 (CA).

[410] *Inverkip Steamship Co Ltd v Bunge & Co* [1917] 2 KB 193 (CA); *Chandris v Isbrandtsen-Moller Co Inc* [1951] 1 KB 240 (CA); *The Delian Spirit* [1972] 1 QB 103 (CA).

However, if the delay causes another type of loss, other than detention of the ship, for example damage to the cargo (which deteriorates), then ship owners can claim unliquidated damages for that other loss.[411]

Lien. A lien is an entitlement to retain possession of property until due payment is made. At common law, there is a lien upon cargo for: freight; general average; and the cost of preserving cargo. GENCON 1994 further provides that 'Owners shall have a lien on the cargo and on all sub-freights payable in respect of the cargo, for freight, deadfreight, demurrage, claims for damages, and all other amounts due under this Charter Party', including costs.[412] Because owners 'shall have' a lien, charterers are under an obligation to procure it (for example, by providing for one in the bills of lading).[413] Laytime and demurrage are not interrupted by the valid exercise of a lien.[414] Nor does it prevent the valid tender of a notice of readiness.[415]

Bills of lading clause.[416] When bills of lading are issued, they are to be on the CONGENBILL form. This form incorporates all terms and conditions, liberties and exceptions of the charter party, including the law and arbitration clause.[417] It

---

[411] *The Eternal Bliss* [2020] EWHC 2373 (Comm).

[412] GENCON 1994, cl 8.

[413] *Fidelitas Shipping Co Ltd v V/O Exportchleb* [1963] 2 Lloyd's Rep 113 (CA).

[414] *The Boral Gas* [1988] 1 Lloyd's Rep 342 (Com Ct).

[415] *Gill & Duffus SA v Rionda Futures Ltd* [1994] 2 Lloyd's Rep 67 (QBD).

[416] GENCON 1994, cl 10.

[417] GENCON 1994, cl 19, whose default position is English law and London arbitration.

has a General Paramount Clause, and also provides for general average to be adjusted according to York-Antwerp Rules in London.[418]

The bills of lading shall be signed by the master, 'without prejudice' to the charter party. This means that the bills of lading do not alter the charter party contract, which remains the governing contract as between ship owners and charterers.[419] There are limits to what bills of lading a master has to sign, for example, not those with incorrect statements of fact,[420] or whose terms are extraordinary or manifestly inconsistent with the charter party.[421] That said, GENCON 1994 provides expressly that charterers are obliged to indemnify owners against all consequences that may arise from signing of bills of lading as presented to the extent that they impose more onerous liabilities than those assumed under the charter party.

---

[418] As is the case under the charter party: GENCON 1994, cl 12.

[419] *Hansen v Harrold Brothers* [1894] 1 QB 612 (CA), 619; *Turner v Haji Goolam Mahomed Azam* [1904] AC 826 (PC); *President of India v Metcalfe Shipping Co Ltd* [1970] 1 QB 289 (CA).

[420] *Compania Naviera Vasconzada v Churchill & Sim* [1906] 1 KB 237 (KBD), 245. Signing a clean bill of lading when the cargo is obviously defective might even be unlawful such that it precludes owners from obtaining any indemnity from charterers: *Brown Jenkinson & Co Ltd v Percy Dalton (London) Ltd* [1957] 2 QB 621 (CA).

[421] *Kruger & Co Ltd v Moel Tryvan Ship Co Ltd* [1907] AC 272 (HL), 278-279; *SS Knutsford Ltd v Tillmanns & Co* [1908] AC 406 (HL), 411; *The Berkshire* [1974] 1 Lloyd's Rep 185 (Adm), 188.

Chapter 10 – Bills of Lading

Transferrable contracts for carriage of goods

Here is a typical series of events. A shipper of cargo will contract with a carrier to take the cargo on board a ship and carry it to a port of destination. Once the cargo is loaded on board the ship, the carrier provides the shipper with a bill of lading. This acts like a receipt, and records what cargo was loaded, and the apparent condition of the cargo. It will also evidence the contract of carriage made earlier between the shipper and the carrier. Meanwhile the shipper sells the cargo to a buyer, and transfers the bill of lading to the buyer. By presenting the bill of lading at the discharge port, the buyer can take delivery of the cargo from the ship. Also, the law deems the bill of lading to contain a contract of carriage between the buyer (as holder of the bill of lading) and the carrier. If the cargo is delivered damaged or short, then the buyer might sue the carrier under the bill of lading.

The bill of lading will often be governed by a regime like the Hague or Hague-Visby Rules, either because those rules are contractually incorporated, usually through a 'clause paramount', or because legislation applies those rules mandatorily.

In this chapter, we will consider the law applicable to bills of lading as it relates to the narrative sketched above, and then we shall discuss key points on the Hague and Hague-Visby Rules.

Bills of lading and transferable contracts

It is the Carriage of Goods by Sea Act 1992 which deems there to be a contract of carriage between the carrier and the lawful holder of a transferable bill of lading.[422] (It creates similar contracts in the case of sea waybills and ship's delivery orders.) 'Transferable' bills of lading are usually those, for example, made out to 'bearer' or 'to order'. What this means is as follows.

On the one hand, a bill of lading might be made out to one named party. This is a 'straight' bill of lading, in which case only that party can present the bill of lading to collect the cargo.[423]

On the other hand, a bill made out 'to bearer' entitles anyone who holds the bill to present it to collect the cargo. Similarly, a bill which is 'S or to order' allows the shipper (S) to indorse the bill, by signing their name, and then hand that bill to another party. If the shipper merely signs their name, then in effect the bill becomes a bearer bill. Or the shipper might also write the name of the indorsee (X). In this case, only X can present the bill – unless the bill was indorsed 'X or to order', in which case X can repeat the process. These latter types of bill allow a cargo to be sold and re-sold while en route, so that the eventual buyer, whoever that turns out to be, can collect the cargo at the discharge port.

---

[422] Carriage of Goods by Sea Act 1992, s 2. The need for a bill of lading to be transferable derives from the statutory definition of a bill of lading in s 1(2).

[423] Nevertheless, the Hague-Visby Rules still apply to a straight bill of lading: *The Rafaela S* [2005] UKHL 11, [2005] 2 AC 423.

The lawful holder of a transferable bill of lading is someone who acts in good faith, and is the bearer of the bill, or is the person in possession of the bill who is identified in the bill as consignee or who has had the bill indorsed to them.[424] As a new transferee gains rights of suit under the bill, previous parties to the contract of carriage lose their rights.[425] However, where the holder of the bill of lading is also the charterer, then any suit will proceed under the charter party (and not the bill of lading).[426]

The lawful holder of a transferable bill of lading can sue the carrier. Who is the carrier? This is usually identified by the signature on the front of the bill of lading (even trumping an express identity of carrier clause on the reverse of the bill).[427] The fallback position is usually to say otherwise that the master signs on behalf of their employer (the ship owner or demise charterer),[428] and they are the carrier, unless it is expressly signed, with authority, on behalf of the charterer.[429]

---

[424] Carriage of Goods by Sea Act 1992, s 5.

[425] Carriage of Goods by Sea Act 1992, s 2(5). This does not happen with sea waybills or ship's delivery orders.

[426] *Rodocanachi Sons & Co v Milburn Bros* (1886) 18 QBD 67 (CA); *The Dunelmia* [1970] 1 QB 289 (CA).

[427] *The Starsin* [2003] UKHL 12.

[428] *Wehner v Dene Steam Shipping Co* [1905] 2 KB 92 (KBD).

[429] *Harrison v Huddersfield Steamship Co Ltd* (1903) 19 TLR 386 (KBD); *The Starsin* [2003] UKHL 12.

Terms of the contract

The terms of the contract contained in the bill of lading might include the Hague or Hague-Visby Rules, or the terms of the charter party under which the bills of lading were issued.

Under the Carriage of Goods by Sea Act 1971, the Hague-Visby Rules shall have the force of law, where there is carriage of goods between ports in different states,[430] if the bills are issued in a contracting state, or if carriage was from a port in a contracting state, or if the contract contained in or evidenced by the bills of lading provides that the Rules shall apply.[431] The latter provision thus gives the Rules the force of law where they are contractually incorporated. Where the bill of lading purports to incorporate the Hague Rules 'as enacted' in the country of shipment, where English law applies, that would be the Hague-Visby Rules.[432]

A bill of lading might seek to incorporate the terms of a charter party. Whether it is successful depends on construing the incorporation clause according to general contractual principles. For example, a clause incorporating the 'conditions' of the charter party did not incorporate exceptions.[433] A clause incorporating the 'terms, conditions and exceptions' of the charter party did not include the arbitration clause.[434] Hence the breadth of the Congenbill bill of lading,

---

[430] Or where the port of shipment is in the UK: Carriage of Goods by Sea Act 1971, s 1(3).

[431] Hague-Visby Rules, Art X; Carriage of Goods by Sea Act 1971, s 1(6).

[432] *The Superior Pescadores* [2016] EWCA Civ 101.

[433] *Serraino & Sons v Campbell* [1891] 1 QB 283 (CA).

118

which provides: 'All terms and conditions, liberties and exceptions of the Charter Party, dated as overleaf, including the Law and Arbitration Clause, are herewith incorporated.' There will be no incorporation of any charter party term which is inconsistent with the express terms of the bill of lading (for example, each having a different rate of freight).[435] Note too that Art III r 8 of the Hague-Visby Rules strikes down any term which purports to give the ship a lesser liability than under the Rules.

The Hague and Hague-Visby Rules[436]

Seaworthiness. Art III r 1 states that the carrier shall be bound before and at the beginning of the voyage to exercise due diligence to make the ship seaworthy. The corresponding exception clause is Art IV r 1, which states that neither the carrier nor the ship shall be liable for loss or damage arising or resulting from unseaworthiness unless caused by want of due diligence on the part of the carrier to make the ship seaworthy. So for example, there is no liability for unseaworthiness if due diligence would not have spotted the problem.[437]

---

[434] *The Federal Bulker* [1989] 1 Lloyd's Rep 103 (CA).

[435] *Gardner & Sons v Trechmann* (1884) 15 QBD 154 (CA). See too: *The Mata K* [1998] 2 Lloyd's Rep 614 (Com Ct), where the charter party 'conclusive evidence' clause was inconsistent with the bill of lading being claused 'weight unknown'.

[436] These two regimes are largely the same. Principal differences are identified below.

[437] *The Yamatogawa* [1990] 2 Lloyd's Rep 39 (Com Ct).

Whenever loss or damage has resulted from unseaworthiness, the burden of proving the exercise of due diligence shall be on the carrier.[438] The duty of due diligence is non-delegable.[439] In other words, it is not good enough that the carrier has reasonably appointed a third party to make the ship seaworthy; if that third party fails to exercise due diligence, then the carrier remains liable. Due diligence is equivalent to the exercise of reasonable care and skill; its absence is negligence.[440]

Care of goods. Art III r 2 states that, subject to the provisions of Art IV, the carrier shall properly and carefully load, handle, stow, carry, keep, care for, and discharge the goods carried. 'Subject to the provisions of Art IV' means that if any loss or damage arises during the loading etc, the carrier can still invoke the exceptions in Art IV. When it comes to activities like loading, stowing, and discharging, the contract of carriage can expressly re-allocate the risk of those activities to another party, like the charterer instead of the carrier, despite the language of Art III r 2.[441] Where cargo is shipped in apparent good order and condition, and discharged damaged, the carrier bears the burden of proving that it took reasonable care under Art III r 2.[442]

---

[438] Hague-Visby Rules, Art IV r 1.

[439] *The Muncaster Castle* [1961] AC 807 (HL).

[440] *The Amstelslot* [1963] 2 Lloyd's Rep 223 (HL).

[441] *Pyrene Co Ltd v Scindia Navigation Co Ltd* [1954] 2 QB 402 (QBD), 417-418; *GH Renton & Co Ltd v Palmyra Trading Corp of Panama* [1957] AC 149 (HL); *The Jordan II* [2004] UKHL 49.

[442] *Volcafe Ltd v Compania Sud Americana de Vapores SA* [2018] UKSC 61.

Exceptions. Art IV r 2 provides a long list of exceptions which the carrier can invoke if it has otherwise failed in its obligation under Art III r 2 to carry the cargo properly and carefully. These exceptions include: act, neglect or default of the master or crew in the navigation or management of the ship; fire;[443] perils of the sea; seizure under legal process; cargo damage arising from inherent vice;[444] insufficiency of packing; and any other cause arising without the actual fault or privity (ie knowledge and acquiescence) of the carrier.

The carrier cannot rely on the Art IV r 2 exceptions if the damage is a consequence of its failure under Art III r 1 to exercise due diligence to make the ship seaworthy before and at the beginning of the voyage.[445] In other words, Art III r 1 trumps. Where loss or damage results from concurrent causes, the ship is only relieved of liability if *all* causes fall within the list of exceptions in Art IV r 2.[446]

Issued bills of lading. After receiving the goods, the carrier shall issue the shipper with a bill of lading showing the identity, quantity, and apparent order and condition of the goods, except where the carrier has no reasonable means of

---

[443] Art IV r 2(b) provides an exception for fire, including fire deliberately or negligently started by (here) the chief engineer, as long as it was without the actual fault or privity of the carrier: *The Lady M* [2019] EWCA Civ 388.

[444] To rely on the exception for inherent vice under Art IV r 2(m), the carrier has to show that the damage occurred despite any reasonable care it took or should have taken: *Volcafe Ltd v Compania Sud Americana de Vapores SA* [2018] UKSC 61.

[445] *Maxine Footwear Co Ltd v Canadian Government Merchant Marine Ltd* [1959] AC 589 (PC).

[446] *The Torenia* [1983] 2 Lloyd's Rep 210 (Com Ct); *Milan Nigeria Ltd v Angeliki B Maritime Co* [2011] EWHC 892 (Comm).

checking, or has reasonable grounds for suspecting their inaccuracy.[447] The 'apparent' condition is its external condition, as it might reasonably appear to the master (for example, whether the cargo was visibly and badly stained).[448] It says nothing about the actual condition of the goods,[449] or the quality of goods, about which the master is not expected to be an expert. At any rate, the shipper shall indemnify the carrier against loss caused by inaccuracies in their description of the goods.[450] If the nature or value of the goods has been knowingly misstated by the shipper, then the carrier is not liable for loss in any event.[451]

The bill of lading is prima facie evidence of receipt of the goods as described.[452] It can become conclusive evidence when the bill of lading is transferred to a third party acting in good faith.[453] However, the presumption has limited effect where the bills of lading are claused, for example, with the common phrase 'weight and quantity unknown'. That makes no representation at all, and so cannot support any presumption.[454]

---

[447] Hague-Visby Rules, Art III r 3.

[448] *Compania Naviera Vasconzada v Churchill & Sim* [1906] 1 KB 237 (KBD).

[449] *The Tai Prize* [2020] EWHC 127 (Comm).

[450] Hague-Visby Rules, Art III r 5. There is no implied obligation on the charterer to indemnify the carrier for any discrepancy between apparent and actual condition: *The Tai Prize* [2020] EWHC 127 (Comm).

[451] Hague-Visby Rules, Art IV r 5(h).

[452] Hague-Visby Rules, Art III r 4.

[453] Hague-Visby Rules, Art III r 4; Carriage of Goods by Sea Act 1992, s 4.

[454] *The Mata K* [1998] 2 Lloyd's Rep 614 (Com Ct).

Just as the issue of a bill of lading raises a presumption, so too does receipt of the goods. Unless notice of loss or damage, and its general nature, be given in writing to the carrier when the goods are removed, or if the loss or damage be not apparent, within three days, such removal is prima facie evidence of delivery by the carrier of the goods as described in the bill of lading.[455]

Limitation of liability.[456] Art IV r 5 provides a limit of liability 'in any event'. This limit shall apply, unless the nature and value of the goods has been declared before shipment and inserted in the bill of lading, or where a higher limit has been expressly agreed. The limit applies even where the loss is caused by the carrier's failure under Art III r 1 to exercise due diligence to make the ship seaworthy.[457] However, under the Hague-Visby Rules (but not the Hague Rules), the carrier cannot invoke limitation where the damage resulted from an act or omission of the carrier done with intent to cause damage, or recklessly and with knowledge that damage would probably result.[458]

Under the Hague Rules, the limit of liability is £100 per package or unit. Reference to 'package or unit' means it does not apply to bulk cargo.[459] The '£100' is measured by the gold value, and so represents a much higher sum in

---

[455] Hague-Visby Rules, Art III r 6.

[456] According to the Hague-Visby Rules, Art VIII, the carrier can also limit liability under the Limitation Convention.

[457] *The Happy Ranger* [2002] EWCA Civ 694.

[458] Hague-Visby Rules, Art IV r 5(e).

[459] *The Aqasia* [2018] EWCA Civ 276.

practice.[460] If goods are shipped in a container, it is the number of packages in the container, rather than the container itself, which is used to calculate the limit of liability.[461]

Under the Hague-Visby Rules, the limit of liability is 666.67 SDRs[462] per package or unit, or 2 SDRs per kilogramme, of the goods lost or damaged, whichever is the higher. Reference to 'goods lost or damaged' means that, where the cargo suffers economic harm, such as a depreciation in value, still the limit of liability is calculated by reference only to physical harm.[463] Where a container is used, the Rules state expressly that the packages or units are those enumerated on the bills of lading as being inside the container, otherwise the container is the package or unit.[464]

Time bar. Art III r 6 states that carrier 'shall in any event be discharged from all liability whatsoever in respect of the goods',[465] unless suit is brought within one year of their delivery or of the date when they should have been delivered.

---

[460] Hague Rules, Art IX; *The Rosa S* [1989] QB 419 (QBD). Under US COGSA, limitation is US$500 per package or customary freight unit.

[461] *The River Gurara* [1998] QB 610 (CA).

[462] SDR = Special Drawing Right, the unit of account of the International Monetary Fund, whose value is determined by a basket of currencies.

[463] *The Limnos* [2008] EWHC 1036 (Comm), [2008] 2 Lloyd's Rep 166.

[464] See too: *Kykuyo Co Ltd v AP Moller-Maersk A/S* [2017] EWHC 654 (Comm), [94], affirmed [2018] EWCA Civ 778.

[465] The Hague Rules have a slightly different formulation: 'In any event the carrier...shall be discharged from all liability in respect of loss or damage...'

Because of the words 'in any event', this time limit will likely apply even where the carrier is in breach of its obligation under Art III r 1 to exercise due diligence to make the ship seaworthy.[466]

It is a substantive time bar which extinguishes the claim or counterclaim or set-off (rather than merely barring the remedy),[467] though it need not preclude a *defence*.[468] Under the Hague-Visby Rules,[469] but not under the Hague Rules, an action for indemnity against a third person may be brought after the expiration of one year.

Claims by carrier. The carrier might sue the charterer under the charter party. The carrier also has a possessory lien at common law over the cargo for general average contributions,[470] and for freight if a common carrier (but not if a private carrier).[471] This is often supplemented by a lien clause in a charter party whose terms might be incorporated into the bill of lading. The carrier can also sue the shipper under the original contract of carriage.[472]

Under the Hague-Visby Rules, the shipper must indemnify the carrier against loss caused by inaccuracies in the description which they furnish of the

---

[466] See too *The Happy Ranger* [2002] EWCA Civ 694.

[467] *The Aries* [1977] 1 WLR 185 (HL), 188.

[468] *The Fiona* [1994] 2 Lloyd's Rep 506 (CA).

[469] Hague-Visby Rules, Art III r 6 bis.

[470] *Castle Insurance v Hong Kong Shipping* [1984] AC 226 (PC).

[471] *Skinner v Upshaw* (1702) 2 Ld Raym 752, 92 ER 3; *Kirchner v Venus* (1859) 12 Moo 361 (PC), 14 ER 948; *Electric Supply Stores v Gaywood* (1909) 100 LT 855 (KBD).

[472] Carriage of Goods by Sea Act 1992, s 3(3); *The Giannis NK* [1998] 1 Lloyd's Rep 337 (HL).

goods.[473] And the shipper is liable for loss caused by the shipment of dangerous goods to which the carrier has not knowingly consented,[474] unless the damage is also caused by the carriers' failure under Art III r 1 to exercise due diligence to make the ship seaworthy.[475] Can duties on the part of the shipper under the bill of lading also be imposed upon lawful transferees? Yes, if the bill of lading holder takes or demands delivery of the goods, or makes a claim itself.[476]

Deviation

Traditionally, if the ship deviates from its voyage, that nullifies any contract of carriage. The carrier becomes a common carrier. It cannot rely on exceptions in the bill of lading.[477] It cannot rely on the exceptions in the Hague Rules.[478] It cannot even rely on the limited common law exceptions available to a common carrier if the damage occurred during the deviation.[479]

    The continuing legitimacy of this rule must be questioned. It is based on the idea that a fundamental breach of contract nullifies the contract, and that theory

---

[473] Hague-Visby Rules, Art III r 5.

[474] Hague-Visby Rules, Art IV r 6.

[475] *The Kapitan Sakharov* [2000] 2 Lloyd's Rep 255 (CA).

[476] Carriage of Goods by Sea Act 1992, s 3. 'Take or demands delivery' means full transfer of possession usually against surrender of the bill of lading: *The Berge Sisar* [2001] 1 Lloyd's Rep 663 (HL).

[477] *Joseph Thorley Ltd v Orchis Steamship Co Ltd* [1907] 1 KB 660 (CA).

[478] *Stag Line Ltd v Foscolo, Mango & Co Ltd* [1932] AC 328 (HL).

[479] *James Morrison & Co Ltd v Shaw, Savill and Albion Co Ltd* [1916] 2 KB 783 (CA).

was rejected decades ago, at least in the general law of contract.[480] It is probably time that the deviation cases be revisited,[481] but it seems that this cannot happen at first instance.[482] Nevertheless, the Rules themselves explicitly permit any deviation in saving or attempting to save life or property at sea, or any reasonable deviation.[483]

Beyond contract

By way of a brief final remark, it is worth noting that a cargo owner might sue the carrier or ship in tort,[484] or in bailment. However, where A bails goods to B with authority to sub-bail, and B sub-bails to C, if A sues C in bailment, C can invoke the terms of the B / C contract in defence.[485] And where a carrier faces a claim in tort, it can invoke any defences available to it under any contract it has with the claimant.[486] The Hague-Visby Rules provide that the Rules shall apply in any

---

[480] *Photo Production Ltd v Securicor Transport Ltd* [1980] AC 827 (HL).

[481] See the discussion in *The Kapitan Petko Voivoda* [2003] EWCA Civ 451, [2003] 2 Lloyd's Rep 1.

[482] *The Sur* [2018] EWHC 1673 (Comm).

[483] Hague-Visby Rules, Art IV r 4. See too *The Al Taha* [1990] 2 Lloyd's Rep 117 (Com Ct), where it was reasonable to deviate for repairs.

[484] *The Bum Chin* [2019] SGHC 143, [2020] 1 Lloyd's Law Rep 130 (Singapore).

[485] *The Pioneer Container* [1994] 2 AC 324 (PC).

[486] *Henderson v Merrett Syndicates Ltd* [1995] 2 AC 145 (HL), 194. Anyway, when a party is under a tortious duty to take reasonable care, surely what is reasonable must be judged against what the parties have expressly contracted for.

action against the carrier in respect of loss or damage to goods covered by a contract of carriage whether the action be founded in contract or in tort.[487]

---

[487] Hague-Visby Rules, Art IV bis r 1; *The Captain Gregos* [1990] 1 Lloyd's Rep 310 (CA).

Chapter 11 – Arbitration: An Outline

Private dispute resolution

We have already encountered a number of arbitration clauses. LOF provides for London arbitration and English law. NYPE provides for arbitration, with a choice between New York under US maritime law, or London under English law, or Singapore under either Singaporean or English law. GENCON also provides for arbitration, with a choice between London under English law, or New York under US maritime law. CONGENBILL incorporates the law and arbitration clause of the governing charter party.

Where there is no express choice of law to govern the arbitration, the law governing the main contract will usually be the implied choice for arbitration also, failing which, the law most closely connected to the arbitration will apply, which is usually the law of the seat (the juridical place of arbitration).[488]

In practice, London is the world's first choice for international arbitration. It hosts more arbitrations than New York, Hong Kong, Singapore and Paris combined. Proceedings under the mantle of the London Maritime Arbitrators Association (LMAA) are the most popular in London, outnumbering other forms of arbitral proceedings and Commercial Court cases combined.

The object of arbitration is to obtain the fair resolution of disputes by an impartial tribunal without unnecessary delay or expense.[489] The law allows that the parties should be free to agree how their disputes are resolved, subject only to such

---

[488] Enka Insaat Ve Sanayi AS v OOO Insurance Company Chubb [2020] UKSC 38.

[489] Arbitration Act 1996, s 1(a).

131

safeguards as are necessary in the public interest.[490] In other words, the parties can choose their own arbitrators, and can agree the procedure to be followed, instead of going to court. The attraction is that the process can be private, flexible, and efficient, and so also prompt and cost-effective, with the parties retaining a large measure of control.

Thus arbitration is concerned with the private resolution of disputes, subject to the oversight provided by the mandatory provisions of the Arbitration Act 1996.[491] This chapter will sketch out the principal provisions of the 1996 Act.

The Act only applies to arbitration agreements in writing.[492] An arbitration agreement is deemed to be separate from any contract of which it forms part.[493] Thus if it is alleged that the main contract is rescinded, the arbitration clause survives as a separate agreement, allowing the tribunal to consider whether the main contract is indeed rescinded,[494] or otherwise invalid.[495] It is similarly possible that the arbitration agreement precedes the finalisation of the main contract, again allowing the tribunal to consider whether the main contract was indeed concluded.[496]

---

[490] Arbitration Act 1996, s 1(b).

[491] Arbitration Act 1996, s 4, and schedule 1.

[492] Arbitration Act 1996, s 5. Arbitration agreements not in writing are outside the Convention on the Recognition and Enforcement of Foreign Arbitral Awards 1958 (New York Convention) – see Art II of the New York Convention. On the enforcement of foreign arbitration awards in England under the New York Convention, see Arbitration Act 1996, Pt III.

[493] Arbitration Act 1996, s 7.

[494] *Fiona Trust & Holding Corp v Privalov* [2007] UKHL 40, [2008] 1 Lloyd's Rep 254.

[495] *The Sea Master* [2018] EWHC 1902 (Comm).

Where parties reach a settlement agreement for money due under a charter party, but do not pay, that dispute can also still be arbitrated. The settlement agreement, although technically a new agreement separate from the charter party, does not oust the arbitration clause, which is meant to govern disputes under the charter party, including disputes about settlement agreements as to sums payable under the charter party.[497] Note, however, that it is possible to commit a repudiatory breach of an arbitration agreement by commencing litigation instead, which repudiatory breach the other party can accept, so terminating the arbitration agreement.[498]

A party can apply to the court to stay legal proceedings in favour of an arbitration agreement.[499] Where Admiralty proceedings are stayed on the ground that the dispute in question should be submitted to arbitration, the court granting the stay may order that any property arrested be retained as security for the satisfaction of the arbitration award.[500]

Arbitral proceedings are commenced by serving notice on the other party.[501] The court may, where just, extend time for bringing arbitral proceedings (even after expiry).[502] However, the court probably cannot extend the one year time bar in the Hague-Visby Rules when those Rules are statutorily applicable.[503]

---

[496] *UR Power GmbH v Kuok Oils and Grains Pte Ltd* [2009] 2 Lloyd's Rep 495 (Com Ct); *Novasen SA v Alimenta SA* [2011] 1 Lloyd's Rep 390 (Com Ct), [52].

[497] *The Four Island* [2018] EWHC 3820 (Comm).

[498] *Marty Ltd v Hualon Corp (Malaysia) SDN BHD* [2018] SGCA 63.

[499] Arbitration Act 1996, s 9.

[500] Arbitration Act 1996, s 11.

[501] Arbitration Act 1996, s 14.

The arbitral tribunal may rule on its own substantive jurisdiction, that is, whether there is a valid arbitration agreement, whether the tribunal is properly constituted, and what matters have been submitted to arbitration in accordance with the arbitration agreement.[504] The parties can object, to the tribunal, that it lacks substantive jurisdiction.[505] The court may determine any question as to the substantive jurisdiction of the tribunal, but only if the application is made with the agreement of all parties or with the permission of the tribunal.[506] Similarly, unless otherwise agreed by the parties,[507] and only with the agreement of all parties or with the permission of the tribunal, the court may determine preliminary questions of law.[508]

The tribunal has various interim powers, for example, to order a claimant to provide security for the costs of the arbitration.[509] The court can also exercise some of its powers in support of arbitral proceedings including, for example, the granting of an injunction.[510]

---

[502] Arbitration Act 1996, s 12. The court can also extend time during arbitral proceedings, by s 79.

[503] *The Antares* [1987] 1 Lloyd's Rep 424 (CA). That case involved the Arbitration Act 1950, s 27, which is worded differently from the Arbitration Act 1996, s 12 – but the latter must be read in conjunction with s 13(4)(a). For a contrary view, see *The Agios Lazaros* [1976] QB 933 (CA).

[504] Arbitration Act 1996, s 30.

[505] Arbitration Act 1996, s 31.

[506] Arbitration Act 1996, s 32.

[507] An agreement to dispense with reasons for the tribunal's award shall be considered an agreement to exclude the court's jurisdiction under this section: Arbitration Act 1996, s 45(1).

[508] Arbitration Act 1996, s 45.

[509] Arbitration Act 1996, s 38.

[510] Arbitration Act 1996, s 44.

When the tribunal makes its award, there are a range of available remedies,[511] including a declaration, or an order for the payment of a sum of money, with interest,[512] or an order that a party do or refrain from doing something, including the specific performance of a contract. It can also award costs.[513] An arbitral award may, by leave of the court, be enforced in the same manner as a court judgment or order.[514]

An arbitral award can be challenged before the courts on three main grounds. In all cases, the challenge must be made within 28 days, and after exhausting all arbitral processes of appeal or review.[515]

First, the award can be challenged on the basis that the tribunal lacks substantive jurisdiction.[516] Second, it can be challenged for serious irregularity which causes substantial injustice.[517] The recognised list of serious irregularities includes failing to act fairly and impartially, and failing to give each party a reasonable opportunity of putting their case.[518] The ability to challenge for substantive jurisdiction or serious irregularity can be lost where the complainant took part in the arbitral proceedings without objection, unless at the time they did

---

[511] Arbitration Act 1996, s 48.

[512] Arbitration Act 1996, s 49.

[513] Arbitration Act 1996, s 61.

[514] Arbitration Act 1996, s 66.

[515] Arbitration Act 1996, s 70.

[516] Arbitration Act 1996, s 67.

[517] Arbitration Act 1996, s 68.

[518] These are among the general duties of the tribunal: Arbitration Act 1996, s 33.

not know and could not with reasonable diligence have discovered the grounds for the objection.[519]

Third, unless otherwise agreed by the parties,[520] there can be an appeal on a point of law, and only with the agreement of all the parties or with the leave of *the court* (not the tribunal).[521] In granting leave to appeal, the court must be satisfied that the question will substantially affect the rights of the parties, and is one which the tribunal was asked to determine. It must also be satisfied that the decision of the tribunal on the question is obviously wrong, or that the question is one of general public importance and the decision of the tribunal is at least open to serious doubt.

Overall, we might say that the general tenor of the Arbitration Act 1996 is to support arbitration, and interfere minimally. After all, the parties have chosen to arbitrate instead of litigate in court.

---

[519] Arbitration Act 1996, s 73.

[520] Once again, an agreement to dispense with reasons for the tribunal's award shall be considered an agreement to exclude the court's jurisdiction under this section. Where the arbitration clause states that the award will be 'final, conclusive and binding', that does not necessarily preclude an appeal on a point of law: *Shell Egypt West Manzala GmbH v Dana Gas Egypt Ltd* [2009] EWHC 2097 (Comm), [2010] 1 Lloyd's Rep 109.

[521] Arbitration Act 1996, s 69.

Select Bibliography

Aikens et al, *Bills of Lading*, 2nd edn (London: Informa, 2015)

Baatz (ed), *Maritime Law*, 4th edn (London: Informa, 2017)

Baatz, 'Clauses paramount', in Soyer and Tettenborn (eds), *Charterparties: Law, Practice and Emerging Legal Issues* (London: Informa, 2018)

Baughen, *Shipping Law* (London: Informa, 2019)

Berlingieri, *Berlingieri on Arrest of Ships*, 6th edn (London: Informa, 2016)

Chiang, 'The Characterization of a Vessel as a Common or Private Carrier' (1974) 48 Tulane L Rev 299

Coghlin et al, *Time Charters* (London: Informa, 2015)

Cooke et al, *Voyage Charters*, 4th edn (London: Informa, 2014)

Cornah, *Lowndes & Rudolf, The Law of General Average and the York-Antwerp Rules*, 15th edn (London: Sweet & Maxwell, 2018)

Derrington and Turner, *The Law and Practice of Admiralty Matters*, 2nd edn (Oxford: Oxford University Press, 2016)

Foxton et al, *Scrutton on Charter Parties and Bills of Lading*, 24th edn (London: Sweet & Maxwell, 2019)

Meeson and Kimbell, *Admiralty Jurisdiction and Practice*, 5th edn (London: Informa, 2017)

Merkin, *Arbitration Law* (London: Informa, 2020)

Merkin and Flannery, *Merkin and Flannery on the Arbitration Act 1996*, 6th edn (London: Informa, 2020)

Rose, *Kennedy and Rose on the Law of Salvage*, 9th edn (London: Sweet & Maxwell, 2017)

Treitel and Reynolds, *Carver on Bills of Lading*, 4th edn (London: Sweet & Maxwell, 2017)

Printed in Great Britain
by Amazon

79386489R00081